W9-BNL-568

# NO JUSTICE

## ONE WHITE POLICE OFFICER, ONE BLACK FAMILY, AND HOW ONE BULLET RIPPED US APART

### ROBBIE TOLAN
#### AND LAWRENCE ROSS

CENTER
STREET®

NEW YORK    NASHVILLE

Copyright © 2018 by Robbie Tolan and Lawrence Ross
Foreword copyright © 2018 by Ken Griffey Jr.

Cover copyright © 2018 by Hachette Book Group, Inc.

Hachette Book Group supports the right to free expression and the value of
copyright. The purpose of copyright is to encourage writers and artists to produce the
creative works that enrich our culture.

The scanning, uploading, and distribution of this book without permission is a theft
of the author's intellectual property. If you would like permission to use material from
the book (other than for review purposes), please contact permissions@hbgusa.com.
Thank you for your support of the author's rights.

Center Street
Hachette Book Group
1290 Avenue of the Americas, New York, NY 10104
centerstreet.com
twitter.com/centerstreet

First Edition: January 2018

Center Street is a division of Hachette Book Group, Inc. The Center Street
name and logo are trademarks of Hachette Book Group, Inc.

The publisher is not responsible for websites (or their content) that are not
owned by the publisher.

The Hachette Speakers Bureau provides a wide range of authors for speaking events.
To find out more, go to www.HachetteSpeakersBureau.com or call (866) 376-6591.

Library of Congress Cataloging-in-Publication Data has been applied for.

ISBNs: 978-1-4789-7665-3 (hardcover), 978-1-4789-7663-9 (ebook)

Printed in the United States of America

LSC-C

10  9  8  7  6  5  4  3  2  1

Dedication...

This book is dedicated to my angels,
TP and Gladys (my grandparents).

Thank you for answering my mom's prayers and
saving my life. I pray that I've done something in this
life and on this earth to make you both proud.

# CONTENTS

# FOREWORD BY KEN GRIFFEY JR.

When Robbie approached me about writing the foreword for his book, my answer was easy. I have known Robbie Tolan since before he was born. His mother, Marian, and my mother are practically sisters, and our dads were teammates in the Major Leagues. In fact, I used to mimic his dad's batting stance when I was younger. His dad, Bobby, and I also share the Comeback Player of the Year Award as members of the Cincinnati Reds. Marian and Bobby Tolan are the godparents of my only daughter, Taryn. As you can see, the Tolan family is indeed very near and dear to me. They are my family.

In 1995, when I broke my wrist, Robbie and his mom were on the first flight to Seattle. Marian helped my wife, Melissa, and me around the house, and Robbie kept my son, Trey, well entertained. For many years Trey was Robbie's shadow; he followed Robbie around the way Robbie followed me around. As a kid, Robbie had such a passion for life. There was always a smile on his face and a light in his eyes indicative of the greatness within him—a greatness that we were all excited to witness. On the night of December 31, 2008, that light went out.

My family and I were absolutely devastated when we received that dreadful phone call in the early hours of New Year's Eve. I called Robbie's phone a dozen times hoping he would answer and tell me that this was all just some sort of sick joke. My heart sank when my family and I were all forced to face Robbie's reality.

Sadly, we all know Robbie's story. Maybe you don't recognize his name or know any specific details of his case. Maybe he hasn't received a lot of publicity, but Robbie Tolan's case is indeed the paramount case in the good fight for righteousness. His is a story that we all hear far too often in this country, especially in recent years. It is a story of grave injustice. It is a story that Robbie and I both heard often as kids, when our dads were not allowed to stay in hotels with their teammates or eat with them at restaurants.

Injustice happens whether we believe it does or not. Here is a man that has dealt injustice a mighty blow. A vast majority of the stories like Robbie's are told posthumously. His life could have very well ended that night in December 2008. In fact, statistically, it probably should have. But thankfully, Robbie is here to tell his *own* story.

Robbie could have been angry and bitter about the hand he was dealt, especially since he was destined to join me in the Major Leagues. And I believe most people would agree that he would have been well within his right to possess those feelings. But the fact that Robbie has made a choice to be happy and joyful and optimistic says a tremendous amount about his character and integrity as a man. He is a man who we can all look up to. Robbie and I talk often, and I am always amazed at his resilience. Robbie is not just a survivor; he is a fighter.

This is undoubtedly an era for change. Robbie Tolan is leading that change. The quest for justice can be a long and lonely one. It is a road that endlessly bends. Robbie has fought for all of us. So let us stand with him, as he stands *for* us. After a good-fought round, let us patch him up in the corner and rub his shoulders before sending him back out to the middle of the ring to fight injustice. And should injustice send him back to us beaten and bruised, let us be his crutch when he is too weak to stand.

I have had a long career in baseball that spans over two decades. The same passion with which I approached my career is the same passion I have for helping Robbie share his story. It is a story that he will have to share for the rest of his life, and I am honored to stand with him to help him do so. So again, when Robbie asked me to write the foreword for this book, the answer was easy; it was an unwavering, resounding yes.

The strongest compliment I can give someone is to consider him or her as family. Well, Robbie Tolan is my baby brother. His spirit and his story will unspeakably touch you. Once you turn this page, you have crossed the Rubicon to this tome that is a triumph for the human spirit. Find out how Robbie is making a difference for present and future generations, and let us go and do likewise.

# NO
# JUSTICE

# CHAPTER 1

# RIGHT PLACE, WRONG LICENSE

**Amadou Diallo, 23, New York, New York—
February 4, 1999**
Four plainclothes New York Police Department
(NYPD) officers killed Bronx resident Amadou Diallo,
a twenty-three-year-old immigrant from Guinea,
outside his apartment. Mistaking Diallo for a serial
rapist, the police compounded their mistake by
misidentifying Diallo's wallet for a gun and shot him
nineteen times. After a trial, the NYPD officers were
acquitted of all charges.

B eing shot.

It's such a unique experience for ninety-nine-point-nine percent of the world who've fortunately never felt a bullet violently enter their body that when people meet someone like me, a person who's actually been shot and lived to tell the tale, well, they kind of want to hear my personal "what-it-was-like-getting-shot" tale. But first, they have questions. Boy, do they have questions.

What did it feel like to have a bullet rip into your body?

Did you think you were going to die?

Did you see a white light?

Is there a heaven?

Is there a hell?

Did you call out for your mother?

Can I see the bullet that's still lodged in your back?

Did you piss yourself?

Were you wearing clean underwear?

Yeah, I've heard all of the questions.

It didn't help that even the well-meaning people in my life inadvertently reduced me from being the person they know—the burgeoning athlete, the happy-go-lucky guy that everyone liked to have around because his personality is so warm, bubbly, and welcoming—to "the guy you read about in the news who took a bullet to the chest." Even my father, the ex-Major League Baseball player Bobby Tolan, mentioned my experience to every single person we met.

*"Did you meet my son, Robbie? He's playing Minor League baseball for the Bay Area Toros. He loves sunsets, little puppies, and helping old people cross streets. And hey, did I mention that he was shot in the chest by a Bellaire police officer last year? Wanna see the bullet? Robbie, lift up your shirt and show the nice woman your gunshot wound. What was that? Oh sure, we'd love to super-size our hamburger order. Thanks for asking."*

The undeniable fact is that I became a celebrity for getting shot by the police, and I hated it. Oh, I didn't hate the celebrity part. As a kid, I'd dreamed about being a celebrity, a sports star that little kids admired and wanted pictures of for their scrapbook, but I never wanted celebrity by painful happenstance like it happened to me. This was a cruel celebrity, where I'd turned into, at least in my hometown of Houston, Texas, a freak show. Nowhere was safe, not even the spaces where I used to feel like I belonged. I was bombarded with questions and requests as "that guy who got shot" from church members, restaurant diners, and even fellow moviegoers.

And being a private person in normal times, I naturally

became paranoid, as I could hear the overly loud whispers from people around me. "Isn't that the guy who got shot?" They'd stare, but ultimately were too afraid to come over to me and ask. I know that most people meant no harm, but it still upset me. I'm a human being. I have achievements and accolades for using my God-given talents, but it doesn't take any talent to be shot, and I'm not proud that I'm the poster boy for being shot by the police. But regardless, Pandora's Box had been opened, and control over how people perceived me was out of my hands because I've found that the public is endlessly fascinated with my story.

Maybe it's because we see so much violence in our media that we're captivated by the details of real-life gunshot victims but fail to recognize the long-term impact being shot has on real-life people.

Gun violence is so cartoonish to us. When Hollywood shoots someone on the big or small screen, the character taking the bullet is typically someone the scriptwriters have convinced us is bad. So after we've spent an hour or two watching their bad acts, we end up *hoping* they'll get what's coming to them in the form of a few slugs to the dome. After all, they wouldn't be getting shot in the first place if they weren't truly bad guys, right?

In my opinion, Hollywood likes making their criminal characters blacks and Latinos—the outsider others in this Land of Freedom, minorities who are by their very existence irrationally scary to good American God-fearing white people (and if you make the villain a Muslim, whoa baby, Katie bar the door, and watch how the bullets fly!).

So guess what? It turns out that you, the viewer, aren't *that* upset when black or brown bad guys get shot by the white hero because you probably thought black and brown people were more likely to be guilty before you ordered your first ten-dollar bag of movie popcorn. And if it's a heroic white *cop* doing the shooting and killing, well that's even better.

*"Do you feel lucky punk? Well...do ya?"*

Remember Clint Eastwood's Harry Callahan? The psychotic 1970s *Dirty Harry* cop character became one of the most popular movie characters of all time after saying that iconic line as he pointed his .44 Magnum, the most powerful handgun in the world, at an injured black criminal's head. What we tend to forget is that earlier in the scene, Eastwood had stood in the middle of the street, blowing away five other black bank robbers, while he never once stopped chewing on his sandwich. No time for that "You have the right to remain silent" bullshit in Callahan's white cop fantasy law-and-order world. Just point, shoot, and sneer as the dead black bodies pile up at your feet.

And audiences cheered for Eastwood's white policeman vigilantism.

They cheered with a sense of righteous indignation that the black bad guys had *finally* gotten what they deserved. No questions. I'm pretty sure white moviegoers would say that they didn't see the color of the criminals, just that they were criminals. That's what Americans do: pretend they don't see race.

"I wouldn't care if the criminal was black, white, or purple," the self-proclaimed nonracist would say, making sure that all of the purple people were accounted for in their anti-racist world." (I always wondered how the purple people felt about being named in the litany of people most people have no prejudices against). "I just wanted to see the criminal get his."

I don't believe these people. Why? Because these weren't just criminals, but *black* criminals, and that made it different. Remember that America had once declared that black folks, as a general principle, had no rights a white man was bound to respect, as Supreme Court Judge Taney said about the enslaved African Dred Scott. So what the hell rights does a black criminal have? His black life doesn't matter, and mine doesn't either.

And that's a crucial concept to grasp if you want to understand my story. How me being shot isn't just some isolated incident, some unlucky circumstance that was an honest mistake that could have happened to anyone. But some people do believe that, mainly because they assume that most white police officers are naturally good when it comes to their interactions with black people. But no, me getting shot wasn't an honest mistake. My being shot is part of a trend that has existed as long as this country has existed. And that leads to another uncomfortable belief about this country we call America:

I think America loves shooting black people.

Yeah, it can be argued that America loves shooting people in general, a sort of *#allshootingsmatter* philosophy, but I'd argue that it particularly enjoys shooting black people. Always has and always will. Even when lynching black people was as common in the United States as picking up a nickel bottle of Coca-Cola at the local five and dime, white Americans regularly riddled the lynched black dead body with bullets as one final exclamation point of violence. It wasn't enough to be dead by hanging; the black body had to be shot, because even dead, the blackness represented an existential threat. And the only power the white people had to extinguish that threat in their white supremacist psyche was to unload as much lead as possible into the dead black body. Often we'd find out *later* that the white people knew that the black person they'd killed had been innocent all along, and still they'd shot the body to pieces with a maniacal glee. Innocence just didn't matter, just like black lives didn't matter.

Not much has changed.

It was the same maniacal glee George Zimmerman tapped into when he killed seventeen-year-old Trayvon Martin, a black teenager who was minding his own business as he walked through an apartment complex to catch the second half of the NBA All-Star game with a bag of Skittles, but Trayvon would die that day at the hands of a white man who thought his black presence on earth needed his personal justification.

America would label the innocent Martin a thug, a scary black menace to white society. They'd turn him into a drug fiend because Martin had the gall to be an American teenager who'd been caught with weed in his school locker. It was as though because he'd been born with black skin, he was a criminal first, with the right to be declared innocent only if he could prove it. Even in death.

*"Do you feel lucky punk? Well…do ya?"*

It was the same glee that cheered when Mike Brown was blown away in Ferguson, Missouri, by a white cop, Officer Darren Wilson. His dead body was left to lie for hours in the middle of the street, given less dignity than that of a dead dog being retrieved by animal services. Earlier, Brown had been seen on video allegedly stealing cigars from a local liquor store, and for that, a lot of white America judged that he deserved the death penalty, even as he knelt with his hands up to peacefully surrender to the police.

*"Do you feel lucky punk? Well…do ya?"*

Tamir Rice, a twelve-year-old black kid playing with a toy gun in a Cleveland park, was shot and killed in less than five seconds after two cops rolled up in a squad car. The white cops would say that Rice was "menacing," and the head of the Cleveland police union would say that Rice was a "twelve-year-old in an adult body." Take a second to let that sink in. Instead of taking responsibility or showing remorse for the tragic death of a child, a grown adult would try to justify the killing of a twelve-year-old kid by saying that he was a big kid.

*Thug. Brute. Criminal.* All gleeful words used to rationalize bullets entering black bodies across the country by police officers. Dead black bodies shot by white police officers spurred the Black Lives Matter movement and protests and the ubiquitous social media hashtags that identified the steady stream of black lives cut short by police violence, but in some corners of America, their killings were enthusiastically encouraged by people who chanted, "All lives matter." I, too, was shot as a result of the same scared white passion for violence against black bodies that Dirty Harry had when blowing away his black perps. I was shot by cops, who, according to recent psychological studies, see "young black men…as taller, more muscular and more threatening than comparably sized white men, a bias that may prompt more aggressive law enforcement response towards them." All of that was going against me, except something different happened when I got shot.

I lived.

And that brings me to the evening that would change my life forever, when I was shot in the chest for doing nothing but existing in this world as a young black man. To the people who would love to criminalize me for my black skin, I want to say this:

9

I was innocent before being shot. I was innocent while being shot. And I'm innocent as I live today. And for all the questions I've been asked, most people miss the ones that I ask myself every day.

What is it like to have your life destroyed in mere seconds?

How do you psychologically, physically, and emotionally overcome nearly dying?

What happens when American society and the criminal justice system turns their back on you and say, "Your black life doesn't matter"?

How do you get over the very real guilt of living through a shooting and the havoc that your continued existence has on the people who love you?

No one knows the answers to those questions except for me. And it's been a ten-year journey into hell for me to find them.

My name is Robbie Tolan, and this is my story.

*   *   *

Bellaire is one of those predominately white bedroom communities you can find anywhere in America. Adjacent to the city of Houston, with its pesky black and Latino inner-city populations, the Bellaire suburb is a testament to the experience of white flight, with high property values, safe streets, and middle-class stability, whereas the black and brown communities in Houston are equated with ghettos, crime, and slums.

A planned community, Bellaire was supposed to represent a slice of pure Americana, with its streets named Holly, Maple, and Pine. There's the ubiquitous Texas small-town water tower that celebrates the Bellaire Little League team, and at one point, the Houston Dynamo Major League Soccer team thought about building a stadium in Bellaire, but ultimately decided against it, having instead built in Houston. Bellaire is a quintessential small town, a place where everyone knows everyone, and with less than 2 percent black people, about 150 black folks in total, it wasn't hard for white people to know who the Tolans were. We were the only African American family on our block.

Our house was located at 804 Woodstock Drive, and it's ironic that the most violent episode of my life would take place on a street named after the 1960s musical festival that's known for peace and love, but that's where it all happened.

A lot of people talk about their neighborhood as being an archetype of the utopian neighborhood from the 1950s television show *Leave It to Beaver*, but my street really could have been a model for that show. Full of modest-sized ranch-style homes, with the occasional two-story brick house, our home could have been a model home for any suburb in Anytown, USA. We weren't rich, but we weren't poor either. We were living the American Dream of being solidly middle class, with middle-class values and middle-class attitudes.

Everyone on my block pretty much had a gardener come by once a week to keep the lawns neat and trimmed, because no one wanted to be *that* homeowner, the one who didn't keep up their house. And as was expected in a neighborhood where streets were named Maple and Elm, trees were everywhere. Besides the trees lining the street next to the sidewalks, most homes also had one or two trees in the middle of their yards. We had three tall majestic trees, each reaching over fifty feet, standing guard over our house like Roman sentinels. To the right of those trees was a one-car driveway that was a short walk to the front door. Our house was right in the middle of the block, with a cul-de-sac about a quarter of a mile down at the end.

As I noted earlier, my father, Bobby Tolan, was an ex-Major League Baseball player, who'd been in the league for a dozen years playing for the St. Louis Cardinals, Cincinnati Reds, San Diego Padres, Philadelphia Phillies, and Pittsburgh Pirates before retiring. He'd been one of the key cogs on one of baseball's all time great teams, the 1967 World Series champion St. Louis Cardinals, a team featuring four future Hall of Famers—Lou Brock, Orlando Cepeda, Steve Carlton, and Bob Gibson.

Athletics is, and has always been, the family business for anyone with any connection to the Tolan bloodlines. It started with my uncle, Eddie "Midnight Express" Tolan, the first African American to be named the "World's Fastest Human" after having won the one-hundred- and two-hundred-meter gold medals at the 1932 Olympic Games in Los Angeles. And as I said, my father had more than a cup of coffee in the major leagues, but he's not even the most famous family member to play baseball. That honor would go to my cousin, the Major League Hall of Famer Ken Griffey Jr.

I was a pretty good athlete at Bellaire High, and I'd played a bit of baseball at Prairie View A&M before heading to the Washington Nationals Minor League system. So yeah, when I hit the football field or the baseball field, I was used to all eyes being on me, to the point that, as a kid, I used to conduct my own "postgame interviews" as a way to entertain myself after playing Little League games, just like my big league idols.

"So Robbie, how do you think you did today?" I'd ask my eight-year-old self in the car after a game.

"Well sir," I'd respond, trying to deepen my voice to approximate the voices of major leaguers I saw on television and people like Tony Gwynn, who we knew as a family friend. "I went three for four, with two home runs and a triple, but I really think that I could have done a little bit better. But we'll get back after them next Saturday."

Everyone, especially my parents, got a kick out of my "interviews," but little did they know that they'd play an important role in how I'd deal with the media when I was truly put in the hot glare of television cameras from around the world. I was mentally preparing myself to answer questions, and I didn't even know it.

But then again, it wasn't like we were looking to be in the spotlight in the first place. We were the quiet black family in town who kept to their own business, never had an issue with our neighbors, and definitely never had any confrontations with the Bellaire police. There might have been one or two times during the fifteen years we'd lived in town when there was a complaint about noise from a party, but nothing serious. In fact, we were quite used to seeing Bellaire police driving up and down our neighborhood blocks, not necessarily to harass, but to serve and protect. Before I got shot, my family thought it was part of the community the police were trying to protect, but au contraire we soon found out. Perhaps if we'd been paying attention, we'd have noticed the warning signs indicating that all wasn't well between the Bellaire police and people of color.

For instance, an incident that was eerily similar to what happened to me six years later happened to a guy named Jose Cruz,

Jr. He'd been stopped by the Bellaire police for a missing front license plate, and on the face of it, that's not much of an issue. The officer gives you a Fix-It ticket warning, you feel good about not getting an expensive ticket for speeding or an illegal lane change, and you go on your own way. It happens a million times a year all across America, except in Cruz, Jr.'s case he ended up arrested and jailed for a night for that missing license plate.

What made Cruz's experience so weird to me is the fact that we have similar backgrounds. An alumni of Bellaire High School like me? Check. Has a dad who was also a former Major League ball player? Check. Jose Cruz, Sr. was a former Houston Astros player and coach and was a legend not only within the club but in Texas baseball in general. The Puerto Rican had been inducted into both the Texas Baseball Hall of Fame and the Hispanic Heritage Baseball Museum. Come from a family of athletes? Check again. His uncles Hector and Tommy Cruz were also long-time Major League baseball players. But none of that mattered when the Bellaire police stopped him.

So why was Cruz, Jr. arrested for a missing license plate, which, he explained as his pregnant wife sat in the passenger seat, was only missing because the car was new? Did he resist arrest? Try to drive away from the scene? Get aggressive in how he interacted with the police officer? Nope. Cruz, Jr. was arrested because the Bellaire police falsely claimed there were warrants out for his arrest, and despite not having *anything* on his record, Cruz, Jr. was handcuffed and taken to jail. You can't be surprised that Cruz, Jr. believed that he was racially profiled. It was a big deal in Bellaire, and despite the apologies from Bellaire officials, Cruz, Jr. never forgot and eventually moved out of Bellaire because of it.

After my shooting incident occurred, a reporter from the *Houston Chronicle* decided to interview some of the 150 black residents of Bellaire and ask them about their experience with the Bellaire police. There was a litany of racial profiling complaints.

One long-time resident, a caterer, had been followed from the grocery store and then verbally abused in front of his children. Earlier, the caterer had been stopped because the Bellaire police claimed that his Ford truck could have been stolen, so they needed to run his plates. It wasn't stolen. It was clear to me that the excuse of a stolen car was the go-to reason for Bellaire police to justify a traffic stop.

In another grocery store incident, a husband and wife had been handcuffed and searched by Bellaire police after a store manager falsely accused them of shoplifting. A black anesthesiologist claimed he was stopped four times in his first year in Bellaire, with the harassment ending only after he went to police headquarters to complain. One story particularly resonated with me because of how absurd it was, and it revolved around something simple: Christmas lights.

One black Bellaire homeowner related the story of one of his black friends, who was putting up Christmas lights on his house one December. What could be more normal? It's the Christmas season, and there are millions of Americans throughout the country untangling lights, climbing up janky ladders, and praying that they're not going to fall and break their necks, all to run up their December electric bill in the name of holiday cheer. Nothing unusual, except in the eyes of the Bellaire police apparently, because when they saw a black man on a ladder holding Christmas lights, they couldn't put two and two together and come to the conclusion that this black man probably owned the house. In other words, the police wanted answers to their unsaid racial prejudices as they stopped in front of the man's house.

"An officer pulled up and asked him what he was doing and if the owner of the house knew what was going on," the black Bellaire homeowner recounted about his black friend's experience. "He told him that he was the owner. He said the cop looked embarrassed and drove off."

What struck me about that experience was that even if you lived in the community and were doing something normal, if you were a person of color, then normal didn't matter. You could still be considered a suspect in the eyes of the Bellaire police. You didn't belong, no matter how much you thought you did. It didn't matter if you stayed out of trouble, paid your taxes, or scored touchdowns for Bellaire High School. If you were black or brown in Bellaire, Texas, you'd better have your papers ready to show to the Bellaire police, or things could turn ugly. I learned just how ugly on December 31, 2008.

My story begins with something rather ordinary: A late-night run to the grocery store. I was back in Bellaire after having played some Minor League ball the previous year as a member of the Bay Area Toros, an independent baseball club out of Texas City, just outside of Galveston Island. I'd done okay that year, but eventually, I asked for my release from the team and headed back home to Bellaire. You don't get rich playing independent baseball, so at twenty-three years old, I was back at my parents' Woodstock house, working a nine-to-five at Pappadeaux's seafood restaurant until the next baseball gig popped up. But it was that nine-to-five that caused me to get into my 2004 Nissan Xterra that fateful night.

I was scheduled to work at Pappadeaux's on New Year's Eve, and knowing that the grocery stores would be closing early and probably running out of champagne, I wanted to make sure that we were fully stocked up by the time I got home. The Tolan family is tighter than tight, and on holidays, we like to get together and celebrate, New Year's Eve being no exception. So my cousin Anthony and I decided to make a quick midnight run to the store.

We stopped off for a game of pool and then got a bite to eat at Jack in the Box before heading back home around two in the morning. We hadn't had anything to drink, and we weren't on any drugs. I want to make that clear because that's almost always the first assumption made during shootings of black people— that we are impaired in some way, so being shot is justified. We weren't impaired.

On our way back home from the champagne run, I hadn't noticed that a Bellaire police car had started following us, but honestly, it wouldn't have surprised me even if I had noticed. As I said before, Bellaire cops were known for cruising up and down the quiet streets of Bellaire, looking for people who didn't belong. Now who those so-called nonbelonging people were was clearly open to a broad interpretation of each Bellaire officer, but let's just say that the Bellaire police department had a long history of interpreting that to mean black and brown people. But having lived in Bellaire for so long, I kind of thought that the police were on my side, you know, doing their best to keep me safe from threats seen and unseen. Everyone knew us. We were the Tolans. We'd lived on Woodstock for fifteen freaking years. We belonged. Or so I thought.

How naïve I was.

It turned out that the Bellaire police were not just doing their routine patrolling; they were on a special mission that night. There'd been a series of stolen cars in the area, and the whole department was primed to catch the culprits. That meant that anyone driving the streets of our little burg was automatically a suspect.

As I turned down Woodstock and parked our car in front of my parents' house, the police were the last thing on my mind. Anthony dropped his wallet and was half-heartedly reaching for it as he talked on the phone with our cousin, Chasen, who was in town from LA. I reached for the bag with the champagne, and as I opened the car door, two bright lights illuminated our car. Before I could make any sense of it, the car sped in front of us, going to the end of the cul-de-sac, where it then turned toward us and turned off its lights.

"Did you see that?" I asked my cousin.

"See what?"

"That car."

"Nah. Help me find my wallet."

And with that, my cousin and I pretty much ignored it, not recognizing that it was a police car. Besides, who cared if it was a police car? We hadn't done anything wrong; no speeding, no illegal turns, no tickets, no warrants for my arrest, nothing. Plus, we were sitting right in front of my parents' house, so why should we think the police were interested in us?

Oh, but how wrong we were. They were definitely interested in us.

Sitting in that Bellaire police car was Officer John Edwards, and Officer Edwards was sure that he'd just caught one of the thieves riding in a stolen Xterra. Turns out that he'd been following us since we'd stopped off at the Jack in the Box for a bite to eat before heading home. As he was driving, he sent in my license plate to dispatch to see if it was a match for one of the stolen cars. The dispatch came back with an answer.

Match.

As Officer Edwards sat in his car at the end of the block, my only interest was getting into the house and getting some sleep; having a confrontation was the last thing on my mind. But Anthony kept fumbling to find his wallet as he stayed on the phone with our cousin.

"Man, let's go," I said, getting frustrated. "Check for it in the morning."

"A'ight," Anthony said, the phone still plastered to his ear.

We got out of the car and made our way to the front door, but neither of us noticed that Officer Edwards had quietly crept his patrol car to the point where it was almost nose-to-nose with the Xterra. As I was about to put the key in the door, I heard Officer Edwards.

"Get down on the ground!"

We turned to see Officer John Edwards pointing his .44 caliber service revolver and a flashlight at us. We were stunned.

"What is happening? Why is this happening?" I thought to myself.

Our brains couldn't make sense of it all. All we did was go to the store, get something to eat, and drive to my parents' house. Why did we suddenly have a gun pointed at us?

There's a scene in the movie *Pulp Fiction* where a nervous robber pulls a gun out on Jules, Samuel L. Jackson's badass character, and Jules coolly says, "Sorry to disappoint you, Ringo, but this ain't the first time someone pulled a gun on me." He wasn't scared. Well, this was the first time someone had pulled a gun on me, and I was scared shitless. My legs started to shake, and I felt my heart rush from my chest to my throat.

"Why? What did we do?" I said, my voice cracking with fear. Instinctually, my cousin and I raised our hands to show that we were not a threat, although Anthony still held his mobile phone in his hand, with my cousin still on the line.

"We had a report of a stolen car."

"What? A stolen car? This is ridiculous. Our car wasn't stolen. Why would he think that? What the hell is going on?" I thought.

"No sir, that car isn't stolen," I said, my voice trying to remain calm and reasonable. The gun was still pointed directly at us. My brain told me I needed to do one thing to stay alive, which was to de-escalate this thing, quickly. They're wrong, but de-escalate this thing. But Officer Edwards wasn't interested in de-escalation. Not in the least.

"That car is stolen! I'm not going to tell you again. Get on the ground right now!"

This is the part where people who've never been in this situation say, "Well, why didn't you just follow the officer's orders and get on the ground?" It's easy to think that, but we were thinking, as citizens, that we had done nothing wrong to deserve this type of treatment. Maybe it's the DNA of Americans, but when we're confronted with an injustice, we all feel that we have a right to speak out about that injustice. And at this moment, at two in the morning in front of my parents' house, Officer Edwards was being unjust. Still, there had to be a better way.

"Sir, this is a mistake. This is my car. This is my house. I live here. I can show you ID."

"I don't want to hear another word. Get on the ground right now!" he barked.

Suddenly, I saw lights turn on inside the house. It was around two in the morning, so I figured that my parents had heard the yelling from inside the house and decided to investigate. But as it happened, my parents had just gotten home themselves, and when they heard us say, "this is my car" they thought Anthony and I were arguing. I could see them coming to the door. "Okay, I'll get down on the ground now because Mom and Dad are about to fix everything," I thought.

I saw the door open, and my dad walked out first, followed by my mom. Both were in their pajamas.

"What's going on?" Dad asked as he stepped out onto the porch. I could see that he was doing a quick survey of the scene and hadn't expected to see the police. When he saw that Officer Edwards had turned his flashlight and gun toward him, he also instinctively raised his hands to show that he wasn't a threat.

"I heard Robbie yelling, 'No, the car is mine,'" my dad recalled about that night. "And I thought he was out there talking to Anthony, his cousin, because they were out there together. So I went outside to stop them from arguing, and that's when I saw this officer with a flashlight, and Robbie was saying that the officer said that they'd stolen the car."

"Listen to this bullshit!" I yelled at my father, livid that it had come to this.

"Robbie, shut up and get on the ground!" my father said, turning back to Officer Edwards, who still had his gun pointed at us. I did what my father said and got on the ground. "What's the problem, Officer?" my dad asked both Anthony and me.

"We have a report of a stolen car."

"No sir. No sir. That's my car," Dad explained calmly. "That's our car. This is my son. That's my nephew. This is our house."

"Get against the wall!" roared Officer Edwards, becoming more belligerent as he rushed toward my dad.

It was as though the officer couldn't believe that he could possibly be wrong, and the more people who questioned him, the angrier he got. But the fact is that he was wrong.

Turns out that while following us, Officer Edwards had incorrectly entered the license plate number. Instead of entering plate number 595BGK, he entered 596BGK, and that wrong plate would unfortunately match a stolen vehicle of the same color and make, but crucially, one model year off. This match caused the squad car's computer to send an automatic message to other police units, informing them that Edwards had found a stolen vehicle.

Getting the license plate wrong was not uncommon, we later found out when we asked a relative who is a cop. Sometimes the cop punching in the license plate is trying to drive and work his dashboard at the same time, and mistakes happen. Because it's so common to get a false hit, most police departments follow a procedure to have their officers double-check the license plate when the car is parked. However, despite parking his police car directly in front of our car, with our license plate clearly in view, as his dash camera would show during future court proceedings, Officer Edwards did not re-check the plate. Instead, he got out of his car, gun at the ready, already convinced that the two black guys in the nearly all-white neighborhood were guilty.

"He should have verified that license plate, which he did not," my dad later said.

"Spread your arms and get up against the truck!" Officer Edwards yelled at my dad. My father immediately complied. While I was lying flat on the ground, I watched as Officer Edwards pushed my dad against our Chevy Suburban, with his gun right at my father's head. He kicked at my dad's feet in order to make him spread eagle.

"He never even really identified himself," my dad remembered. "Since he was a law officer, he could have asked me for ID, or the registration of the car, and this could all be resolved. But he never did that. To me, he was just in a hurry to do something that would make a name in his police department.

"You would think that any reasonable good police officer would have said, 'Sir, let me explain what's going on. We got a report of a stolen car and it fits this description. But he didn't do that. I think he was more interested in making a bust, as I think that's how they get promoted in their department."

"What the fuck is going on?" I thought, sweat now dripping down my face and into my eyes. I could hear my mother plead for the officer to listen to us, to think about what he was doing.

Officer Edwards was having none of it. And when his backup arrived, Sergeant Jeffrey Cotton, things went from bad to worse.

Sgt. Cotton is one of those cops who, if you're black, you dread meeting at a traffic stop. Why? Because at first glance, Cotton represented the white American ideal of a cop. He had a blond close-cropped military haircut and a powerful body-builder physique. He was a police officer who seemed to be looking for action wherever he could find it. And he soon found it.

Anthony was trying to keep the phone on his ear so our cousin could hear what was going on, and at the same time, my mother was trying to make sure nothing happened to us. She grabbed Anthony's phone, while trying to figure out why this was happening. Because of the commotion, no one had seen or heard Sgt. Cotton drive up, and without identifying himself, he came from behind our SUV and immediately escalated the situation.

"Get up against the wall!" Sgt. Cotton yelled at my mother.

Startled, she couldn't believe that he was talking to her. Where did he come from?

"Are you kidding me? We've lived here fifteen years. We've never had anything like this happen before," my mom said, turning to Cotton.

Sgt. Cotton didn't care. He grabbed my mother, a fifty-five-year-old woman, and threw her like a rag doll against the garage door. You should understand that my mother is not a big woman at all. She's a tiny petite woman, who even in the most warped fantasies couldn't threaten or harm anyone. So when Cotton grabbed her and flung her to the garage door, it was like he'd lifted her body off the ground.

That's when I snapped. There was something about seeing my mother being abused that instinctively made me want to protect her—protect her in the same way that she wanted to protect me.

"Get your fucking hands off my mother!" I shouted as I slowly rose from the ground, my hands and arms still spread wide. I never did stand up, because as I rose to one knee, Sgt. Cotton turned, aimed his .45 down at me, and fired at my chest.

Boom.

My mother said that she was so close to the gun that she could see the fire from the gun as the bullet headed toward me at over eight hundred feet per second. Cotton fired three times, and one of the bullets hit my chest, right under my right nipple.

I couldn't believe it, even as I flew back into our front door from the impact. Had he shot me? Maybe it was a beanbag? Maybe it was a rubber bullet? Maybe it was something else, but it couldn't be a bullet, right? It couldn't have been real. I slumped against the front door and slowly slid down to the ground.

"Oh my God, I can see smoke coming from his chest!" my mother screamed, as she saw the damage the bullet had done to my body.

"That's just smoke from the fibers of his clothes," Sgt. Cotton said, as casually as one would say that he likes ketchup with his fries. He appeared to be unbothered as I sat there dying, although he would say something very different during the trials.

I tried to get up, but it felt like I had the weight of a ten-story building on my chest, with over two thousand pounds of brute force compressing my chest. I wanted to cry out, to say something, but I couldn't. I reached under my t-shirt and then looked at my hand. My hand was smeared with blood.

Gasping for air, thoughts rapidly rolled through my brain. What I didn't know is that the bullet had ripped through my right lung and had damn near liquefied my liver. In the distance, I could hear my mother scream, and then her desperate prayers.

"Please Lord, keep your healing hands on my son!" my panicked mother shouted over and over as I struggled to maintain consciousness. I thought I was going to die, and if you think that you don't need the help of prayer in your efforts to stay alive, you're a damn fool.

I tried to say the Lord's Prayer, but the only thing I could do was say, "Our Father…Our Father…" because I could feel my breath leaving me, but none coming back into my body.

When you think that you're going to die, you don't have some sort of peaceful wave wash over you. That's Hollywood bullshit. In reality, thoughts of impending death are one of the ugliest, most brutal experiences you can have. All of the horror films in the world can't prepare you for being that scared. And as my body slid down to the ground, forever violated by Cotton's bullet, I could feel a combination of panic and helplessness overcome me, as I was suddenly in the hands of strangers to keep me alive, specifically and initially, the Bellaire Police Department and the city's emergency medical technicians (EMTs) in their ambulances. The people who tried to kill me, or people connected to the people who tried to kill me, were the ones tasked with keeping me alive. As my cousin Anthony would later joke, "Where they do that at?"

The EMTs and more Bellaire cops arrived, and as I struggled to maintain consciousness, I saw various officers putting my family—my family who'd just minutes before been minding their own business—into handcuffs like common criminals. Anthony, my mother Marian, and my father Bobby were all shackled like they'd done something wrong, and they were put in the back of separate police cars. My father, in the back of his own police car, heard as the truth was coming over the radio.

"While I'm in the police car," my dad recalled, "I can hear the police dispatcher say that the car wasn't stolen, so I'm pounding on the glass trying to get their attention. One lady officer on the outside turned to me with a look on her face that said, 'Just shut up.' If I could have kicked that window out, I would have."

In the back of another police car, my mother, in a panic after having seen her baby shot at point-blank range and not knowing if I was going to live, continued to pray.

"Please Lord, keep your healing hands on my son!"

"Keep quiet," a Bellaire officer ordered, as she glared at my mother.

The EMTs rushed to strap me onto a gurney and put me into an ambulance, but I remember one of them looking me directly in the face and asking, "What happened to you?" Before I could answer, Sgt. Cotton responded, "Don't worry about what happened to him."

As the EMTs lifted me into the ambulance, I could see Sgt. Cotton huddled with other officers, some who had not been at the scene when I was shot, and I specifically recall him saying, "Okay, people are going to start showing up. We've gotta get our stories straight."

That's when I knew that it was going to be me against the Bellaire Police Department and the City of Bellaire.

As the ambulance took me to the hospital, I remember telling the EMTs, "No, no, no, I need my parents. Someone get my parents." And yet, no one did anything. Instead, they were cutting my shirt off and putting monitors on my chest. They were doing stuff, but I was panicking because I knew that I was dying and I just wanted my parents to be there with me. But they kept pushing me back down on the gurney, and that's when I thought that I'd never see my parents again.

The ride to the hospital was one of the worst in my life. I felt every bump, every jolt, as my breathing became more labored. Strangely, though, as the ambulance arrived at Ben Taub General Hospital, I felt calm come over me. True, the burning sensation of the bullet traveling through my body, as a violent foreign interloper into my being, hadn't dulled. But mentally, I put my life into the hands of the people at the hospital who rushed toward me. The further away I was from the Bellaire police, the more I felt as though the people surrounding me wanted me to live. I was tapping into a faith that these humans were righteous and ready to do good.

Just like in the movies, as the gurney whipped through the hospital hallway toward the operating room, I stared up at the faces of multiple nurses, each asking questions, clipboard in hand.

"You're going to be just fine. What's your name? What's your Social Security number? Do you take any medicines?"

"Robbie Tolan. My Social Security is . . . ."

I shook my head as each question came, barely understanding them. I just wanted the pain to end. They took my new shoes off, cut my pants off, and hooked me up to an IV. I was still terrified; nothing like this had ever happened to me before. Finally, as we arrived at the operating room and they lifted me onto the table, it dawned on me that I might not fucking come out of this.

I could actually die from driving my own car and walking to my own house in my own neighborhood. And no one but my family would care.

I was scared to death and I wanted my mom. There I was, a grown man, needing my mom in the same way I needed her when I was a kid and fell off my bike. It's something primal, and I heard that it happens all the time in war, when even the most grizzled veteran calls out for his mother when shot. Your brain, I think, searches for comfort and safety in times of imminent danger, and the essence of that comfort and safety tends to come from your mom. I knew that I might be dying, and I felt like having her with me would make it better. But she wasn't there, and as a result, I felt intensely alone.

It was then that the anesthesiologist slid a clear mask over my face, tightening the bands around my head.

"Breathe deeply, Robbie, and count down from one hundred for me."

"One hundred. Ninety-nine. Ninety-eight. Ninety-seven...."

All of the sudden, the pain from the gunshot and the world around me faded into the distant reaches of my consciousness as the anesthesia gradually did its work. I was still scared, but I was also at peace. And peace was all that I wanted at that point. Peace.

# CHAPTER 2

# MY NEW REALITY

**Sean Bell, 23, New York, New York—November 25, 2006**

Sean Bell, a twenty-three-year-old African American man, was shot over fifty times by five New York uniformed and plainclothes police after leaving his bachelor party at Club Kalua, a strip club. The police had targeted the strip club for prostitution and was intending to raid it when they encountered Bell and his three friends leaving the club. According to the police, Bell attempted to strike an officer with his car when officers opened fire on the car, killing Bell and severely wounding two others. Three of the five NYPD officers were charged with first- and second-degree manslaughter, second-degree reckless endangerment, and first- and second-degree assault. They were subsequently acquitted on all charges.

Wake up, Robbie. Wake up, baby."

As I struggled to release myself from the grips of the drugs after surgery, my ears heard the soft pleadings of my mother, but still, I kept my eyes closed. I wanted a few moments of listening to her loving words before I had to deal with the harsh realities of my near-death experience. I took comfort in the fact that I could feel her squeeze my hand as she spoke.

When I finally opened my eyes, my first thought was that I had to be dead. There was a bright light shining in my eyes, and I thought to myself, "Wait, is this the bright light everyone talks about when you die?"

No, I wasn't dead. And yes, it's kind of funny now when I look back on it, but after turning my eyes away from the lamp above me, I saw that I was surrounded not only by my mother and father, but seemingly every aunt and uncle I had on this planet.

They spilled out of my small hospital room and into the hallway, and I was so relieved because I never thought I'd see them again.

"What happened?" I asked finally, as my eyes darted around the hospital room, trying to make sense of where I was. My mother, who was in tears, came over and gave me a kiss and sang praise to God, while my father had that stoic look of a dad coming to the awful realization that he hadn't been able to keep his child safe and now was helpless to do anything except watch his son deal with the pain.

I knew that I'd been shot, but everything else had become hazy from the moment I'd entered the hospital. How long had I been knocked out? What day was it? Was I going to live or die? Did they get the bullet? Would I play baseball again? Nothing seemed to be normal. I still had trouble breathing, with the pain of the bullet that ripped through my right lung never leaving me despite the drugs.

As the hospital monitors buzzed and beeped, the anesthesia made my eyes feel heavy, but I was afraid to close them. I might not wake up.

"Do you remember anything?" my mother asked, the concern lining her face. I hesitated, and I'm not sure if she was relieved or petrified. I could remember certain details, but not everything.

My family then frantically tried to explain what happened from their different points of view, trying to fill in my blanks. What they didn't know was that it was too much for my brain to handle.

"You were in surgery for about four hours," one voice said.

"I think that Cotton shot at you three times because there are two other bullets in the house," another voice said.

34

"They wouldn't let Tammy and Chasen into the house after we were taken away in the police cars, talking about that it was a crime scene. When we asked them what crime was committed, they just walked away," said yet another.

"Anthony was made to give statements to the police like he'd committed a crime."

"Do you remember that after you were shot, Cotton started going through your pockets? He kept saying, 'What were you reaching for?'"

All of their voices quickly turned into one massive mumble, resembling the indistinct voices of Charlie Brown's parents. As I lay in the hospital bed, with the antiseptic white walls closing in on me, I felt like I was alone, even though I was surrounded by people who loved me. I felt like they were trying to give me key pieces to a puzzle, but no matter how many pieces they put in my lap, I still didn't have the picture on the box to make sense of it all. Plus, to be honest, I didn't want to talk about it. This was an extraordinarily traumatic event, and I'd moved from thinking that I was going to die to enjoying the fact that I was still alive.

The one thing I did note, though, was how my dad said the police treated him after releasing him. Remember, he'd been in his pajamas when he'd gotten to the hospital, so he needed to go back to our house and change. But when he got there, the police had yellow taped the front door and said that he couldn't enter because he'd be contaminating a crime scene.

My dad said a police officer told him he could crawl through a back window if he wanted to get inside. "The guy thought it was like a joke. Meanwhile, I'm seeing them walk back and forth through the front door with no issues."

As everyone continued to talk around me, my eyes eventually moved from them to the television, where it turned out, unsurprisingly, that I was the lead news story.

"Questions surround the shooting of baseballer's son...."

"Bellaire police very tight-lipped over shooting...."

"Tolan is one of three black men shot by white police officers in the past twenty-four hours of this New Year's holiday, two of them dying. Inquiries are being made...."

Wait, what? I thought. Two other black men had been shot? Where? What happened? It turns out that the twenty-four hours between 2008 New Year's Eve and 2009 New Year's Day had turned into a particularly busy time for white officers shooting black men.

One guy, Adolph Grimes III, was one of the thousands of Hurricane Katrina victims who'd moved from New Orleans to Houston, and if you go by the history of the Bellaire police, Grimes was the exact type they'd harass if he showed up driving down one of our tree-lined streets. But in this instance, Grimes was back in New Orleans, visiting relatives for the New Year's holiday, when nine New Orleans cops, in a situation that was eerily similar to my own, gunned him down.

Grimes had driven from Houston to New Orleans, a five-hour trip, and according to his father, he had gotten there right around midnight, "without a second to spare" before the start of the new year. All was good as the Grimes family celebrated New Year's at his grandmother's house right outside the French Quarter. However, as the celebratory fireworks exploded over New Orleans, things took a horrible turn around three o'clock in the morning.

As Grimes walked from his grandmother's house to his car, waiting for his cousin to come out, nine undercover narcotics officers unexpectedly surrounded his car, guns drawn. The New Orleans narcotics team had been out on patrol that evening, in the same way that Bellaire cops were on patrol looking for the crew stealing cars. They'd locked on Grimes, even though he hadn't been doing anything criminal. What happened next is up for debate.

According to the New Orleans police, Grimes shot at them and then ran. The Grimes family maintains that Grimes was simply running for his life, knowing the reputation of the New Orleans police. Or, they thought that maybe Grimes believed he was going to be robbed since the police were in plainclothes.

To the New Orleans police, Grimes was a dangerous suspect who needed to be stopped. Regardless of which side you take, the undeniable fact is that nine New Orleans cops shot at Grimes forty-eight times, hitting him fourteen times, including twelve shots to the back. And yes, Grimes had a gun, but he had a legal permit to carry the firearm.

Like me, Grimes had no criminal record, had gone to a prestigious high school in his hometown, and was just outside his own family's house when he was shot. He was twenty-two years old, just a year younger than me, and although I have no children, I feel for him because he had a seventeen-month-old son who will never know his father. There were so many similarities between Grimes and me that it freaked me out.

The third black victim of those twenty-four hours, twenty-three-year-old Oscar Grant, was shot in Oakland. I watched the report about his killing, but the impact only hit me days later when the explosive video of his murder was released. And again, there were similarities to my incident.

The Oscar Grant shooting took place around two o'clock in the morning on New Year's Day. Grant and his friends were taking the Bay Area Rapid Transit (BART) subway train from San Francisco to Oakland, after celebrating New Year's with others, when the BART police were called about a possible fight between some riders who were "hammered and stoned" on the train. When the BART train arrived at the Fruitvale Station in Oakland, two BART officers took Grant and his three friends off the train and promptly put them up against the wall, handcuffing one. One of the officers punched one of them, agitating the other passengers on the train, and that's when things started going sideways.

Just like how Sgt. Cotton arrived on the scene to make a bad situation worse, BART officer Johannes Mehserle arrived at the Fruitvale Station scene late and attempted to handcuff Grant. Grant had been forced to the ground, just like I had been, face down, but when he heard that he was going to be arrested, he tried to raise himself up. Officer Mehserle put a knee in his back, forcing him to stay on the ground.

All of this was being recorded by other passengers with cell phones because they were skeptical of any interaction between black men and cops as a result of the nationwide epidemic of white cops shooting black men. So it had become routine, almost a necessity, to pull out a phone and record the police interactions, just like Anthony had tried to keep my cousin on the line during our own incident.

Meanwhile, as Mehserle pulled on Grant's right arm and hand, trying to get handcuffs on him, he kept yelling at Grant to comply.

"Don't taze me," Grant kept repeating. Suddenly, Mehserle stood up, unholstered his semi-automatic handgun, a SIG Sauer P226, and shot Grant in the back, with the bullet exiting Grant's chest and ricocheting on the concrete platform.

"You shot me! I got a four-year-old daughter!" Grant shouted, a passenger recalled. Seven hours later, Grant died at Oakland's Highland Hospital, a hospital so well known for dealing with gunshot wounds that the military sent its own doctors to Highland to see how they treated bullet wounds for their own work treating combat injuries.

Three black men, either my age or close to it, shot in less than twenty-four hours, and here I am, miracle of all miracles, still alive while they are dead. I didn't know it at the time, but this was the beginning of my feelings of guilt at having lived. Mentally, nothing can prepare you for the guilt; it just comes at you, and when it comes, it comes hard and strong.

*    *    *

"I knew you were different when you arrived."

"How?"

"Your shoes. When you came in, I looked down at your shoes and thought 'Man, those are some expensive shoes.'"

The chief of staff at Ben Taub General Hospital, Dr. Kenneth Mattox, is the unsung hero in my story, just one of many people who used their intuition to realize that I hadn't done anything to deserve getting shot.

It's strange to think that we have categories of people who deserve and who don't deserve to be shot, but we do, mainly because of the consistency of the people who are brought into the trauma unit on their backs, bleeding and holding onto life, and they ain't a bunch of white hedge fund managers.

Dr. Mattox said that most of his gunshot victims were from the inner city, and you could identify them by their dress: baggy clothes, tattoos, and gaudy jewelry. I didn't fit that description, so it struck him as odd that I was in his operating room. Not that the young men and women who *did* wear the uniform of the inner city deserved to be shot by the police, but I stood out as an exception.

According to Dr. Mattox, the Bellaire police had wanted to follow me into the operating room, get the clothes they'd cut off me as evidence, and then interrogate me after my surgery, but he wouldn't allow it. He ran his hospital the way he wanted, and he wasn't about to have his patient handcuffed to the bed if he thought the patient hadn't done anything wrong.

"I didn't think those guys from Bellaire were up to any good, especially after they tried to barge in my operating room and demand my staff to give them your clothes that we cut off of you."

Dr. Mattox gave me a code name, Unknown 90, as a way to throw the Bellaire police off my location in the hospital. He put me in a private room and then let my family use a conference room to get away from the police. Hiding a patient was something that hospitals did when they had a celebrity in residence, and it kept the media at bay. This was the first indication that I'd become a celebrity of sorts for taking a police bullet.

"So I have some good news and some bad news," Dr. Mattox told me and my parents, as the rest of the family left the room.

"The good news is that you're going to be just fine," he started.

"You're a baseball player, right? Well, you'll be able to do everything you did before you were shot."

"And the bad news?" I asked, as I tried to lift myself slowly in the bed to a sitting position. Every movement hurt.

"The bad news is that we had to leave the bullet in your liver," he said.

"What?"

"It was too dangerous to try to take out," he said. "We think that if we'd tried to take it out, you would have bled out. But here's the thing: your liver will function just fine. In fact, it will heal around the bullet."

I had to let that sink in. I now had a bullet inside my body for the rest of my life, for the crime of doing nothing except going home. One minute, I was fine. The next, I had a bullet in my liver for doing nothing. What type of world was I living in? I knew I would have plenty of time to contemplate that question, but first, I had to survive the aftermath.

Life in the hospital wasn't comfortable at all. Pain was everywhere in my body, at all times. Everything the doctors and nurses did to get me healthy revolved around that pain, and I swear that pain is seared into my soul.

The nurses had inserted an NG tube, a plastic tube that goes through the nose, past the throat, and down into the stomach, used to provide nutrition and administer medicine. The NG tube made talking difficult, but it also made me constantly thirsty, as the tube filled my throat. When the nurses weren't looking, I'd get sips of water from my relatives. I don't know if that was a bad thing; okay, yeah, I know that was a bad thing, but it didn't ultimately kill me, so hey...

Obviously, the bullet left a gaping hole in my chest, and that required my nurses to pack the wound with medicated gauze. The doctors explained that they couldn't sew up the wound because it would have healed on the surface, but then would have become infected underneath the surface. Unfortunately, that meant that the gauze needed to be changed each day, which was my least favorite routine, as the nurse would first use a cotton swab to pack the gauze deeply into the wound. It was beyond painful. But it wasn't as painful as when the nurse had to come back later to pull it out with a pair of pliers, which made me feel like my chest was being ripped wide open. The doctors required that the gauze be changed twice a day, every day, and it was something I dreaded deep in the marrow of my bone. But that was just the beginning of my life of pain.

Six inches under my right armpit, a chest tube had been inserted through the ribs and into my liver, draining all of the blood and puss from my liver and causing the small bag hanging on the side of my bed to look like a Halloween prop. It also meant that my arm was constantly in the air because to bring it down meant extreme pain. Try keeping your arm in the air for five minutes. Now do it for ten minutes. Now imagine keeping your arm in the air for days on end. That was my life.

Now, to get to the bullet, the surgeons had to make an incision from the bottom of my sternum to an inch and a half past my belly button; the incision was held together by thirty-eight staples. My breathing was already labored, but with the staples, it felt like each breath was pulling at the incision, so there was constant pain.

Needless to say, I was jacked up on so much anesthesia,

morphine, and Vicodin for most of my early stay in the hospital that I was woozy to the point that when I had visitors, I'd engage for a few minutes and then completely crash from exhaustion. Soon the nurses put me on an intrathecal pump, a tube inserted into my spinal column that, with a push of a button, injected me with morphine. The pain was so bad it would wake me up, so I found myself pushing the button ten times, hoping that I'd get a larger dose of morphine, even though the pump prevents patients from getting more than they are allowed.

Because the bullet had caused my lung to collapse, Dr. Mattox ordered me to cough as often as possible as a way to re-inflate the lung. Sometimes, he'd pop in just long enough so that I'd cough, and just his seeing his head in the door caused me to have a Pavlovian response.

But, like everything else in my life, even coughing was complicated. The problem was that while I was in the hospital, I developed a mysterious pain that doctors could never explain or identify but that was, unfortunately, triggered by my coughing. Every time I coughed, it felt like I was being tasered, hard, and it lasted for months after I left the hospital. So here I was. On the one hand, I wanted to breathe, but on the other hand, breathing came with a painful price.

Great.

Oh, and let's not forget the sticking of the needles. The nurses were always taking my vitals, making my veins raw and weak, so it would sometimes take up to thirty minutes to find a good one. One time, I was poked eight times before the nurse decided to turn over the job to an IV technician. It got to the point that any time the nurse entered my room to draw blood, I'd convulse in tears. I was a grown man who'd become fearful of a needle, like I was a three-year-old child going to the doctor.

My previously athletic and muscular body swelled up like a fat balloon, partly because moving was so difficult. Walking from the bed to the bathroom was a huge challenge, so a week after I'd been shot I gained over 30 pounds, going from 205 pounds to 240 pounds. That, no matter how you measure it, was not good. To keep my body from swelling, the nurses wrapped two cuffs around my ankles that were designed to compress every thirty minutes, which also helped prevent blood clots. The bed inflated and deflated to keep the blood circulating throughout my body as much as possible.

All of the constant excruciating pain started to affect me mentally. I began having panic attacks. I was trapped in a body that I didn't understand and didn't recognize, and my brain couldn't comprehend how to deal with it. It was as though it didn't know whether the pain would ever go away, and I'd be trapped like this forever.

One night, I woke up in a panic from a nightmare, and the only thing I could see were all of these wires, tubes, monitors, and machines beeping and pulsating, and I freaked out. I ripped the NG tube out of my nose, and for just a minute, I felt relief. I finally felt like I was in control of my body and my life.

However that control was an illusion, and reality came back to me quickly. The reality was the painful process of putting the NG tube back into my nose; one nurse held my head back and another shoved the plastic tube through my nostrils, like I was a torture victim.

Even when I received good news, like when one of the tubes

was removed because I'd improved, the pain was never far away. But believe me when I say that nothing compared to the pain that was to come when my chest tube was removed. And it came all of a sudden.

I was minding my business and talking with my family when two doctors burst into my room like they were part of a SWAT team.

"Everyone needs to leave. Now!"

Whoa. My eyes started darting around as I tried to figure out what the hell was happening. You could tell that the doctors were not playing around, not at all, and I guess that the shock-and-awe approach was designed to create a sense of authority so that no one even thought to question them. It was effective because everyone left the room like their pants were on fire.

"What's going on?" I asked frantically. No one said anything, but they both raised my arm above my head.

"Close your eyes and take a deep breath and hold it. When you do it, close your lips."

Sorry, but the only thing going through my head was one phrase: What the fuck?

At this point, I was beyond panicky. What the hell was going on? But I did as I was told because doctors sorta have that effect on you.

As soon as I closed my lips, that was the signal for them to pull out my tube, and they did. It probably only took a second, but it felt like an eternity. The pain was intense, and the sound of the tube being removed sounded like a person shoving a hand into a bowl of wet noodles.

Not good.

Being in the hospital made me feel like I was living in a cage. I'm naturally a physical guy. I'm used to moving and moving with a purpose, and here I was tied to a damn hospital bed. My hospital stay lasted three weeks because I needed a lot of physical therapy, which didn't go that well in the beginning. I literally needed about thirty minutes to walk four steps. My body was in such bad shape, with swollen areas everywhere, that simply opening my eyes to start a new day was discouraging. I started to lose hope, and when you start losing hope, it's hard to mark progress.

Once the swelling went down, I was able to get around a little bit better. I walked with a walker sometimes three or four times a day, with two people on each side of me and one in back of me, just in case I fell back. I had to walk because the doctors said that if I didn't, they might have to do another surgery due to fluid building up in my liver, and I didn't want another surgery. Thankfully, the walking worked to reduce the fluid.

I'm not telling you all of this to gross you out or gain your sympathy. That's not my intention. I want people to understand that a single bullet does profound damage to the body, and although the scars may heal, the trauma never really does. You live with the pain, the memory of the pain, and the mental baggage that comes with it forever. That's the constant drumbeat in my life as I deal with the pain, and it's not fair. And we need to do something about it.

Why? Because the facts of my case are simple, at least in my eyes, when it comes to how unjust my shooting was. I was driving my own car. I was parked in front of my own house. I was not armed. I was not drunk or high. I didn't have a record. And I was shot because of the incompetence of two police officers who didn't have the foresight to double check a license plate. I don't know how you can spin that in favor of the police.

In essence, I was shot for no reason, but that didn't stop the Bellaire authorities from trying to convince the media and the public that race had nothing to do with Anthony and I being stopped in the first place. It defied logic.

"Anytime someone is injured, we take it very seriously," Byron Holloway, Assistant Chief of the Bellaire Police Department, told the *Houston Chronicle*. "But any allegation of racial profiling, I don't think that's going to float."

I don't think that's going to float. Holloway didn't even pretend that he was going to take a look into the *potential* of racial profiling. He just dismissed it out of hand, based on his "thoughts."

At least the mayor of Bellaire, Cindy Siegel, was a bit more circumspect.

"Am I going to say there's no racial profiling?" she asked rhetorically. "I don't know. But if we've got a problem, we're going to fix it. There's no place in city government for treating people differently based on race or sex."

That said, Siegel told the *Houston Chronicle* that she'd never seen anyone come to her with a racial profiling allegation, even though she did remember one couple that had been accused of shoplifting at a Bellaire supermarket. Talk about having a blind spot to the lives of black people in your city. Just one anecdotal story is all you remember?

Look, I'm not an expert on how to run a city government or lead a police department, so hey, sue me if what I'm saying is out of bounds. But wouldn't you, as a mayor or an assistant police chief, go to a few conferences with other mayors and police departments and sit in on a few workshops devoted to the problem of racial profiling? And hey, even if you didn't think that Bellaire had a problem, you'd be proactive by maybe conducting a study about the matter, even if it was simply to keep up appearances, right?

To me, that would seem to be a rational way to run a city and a police department, but apparently, both Holloway and Siegel operated under the "see no evil, speak no evil, hear no evil" philosophy as part of their public policy strategy. If you don't go looking for racial profiling, then it must not exist.

Fortunately, the NAACP, who actually does study racial profiling across the country, thought differently.

"Bellaire has a perception that they are a racist community, and...that is not something we want in the Houston area," Executive Director Yolanda Smith said at a news conference right after my shooting. "There is the perception for African-Americans and Hispanics that for whatever reason there are rogue cops...that this is a place you don't want to go into because the police target [minorities]."

Dr. D. Z. Cofield served as the Senior Pastor of the 144-year-old Good Hope Missionary Baptist Church and was also the vice president of the Houston branch of the NAACP.

"While this perception is prevalent about the Bellaire Police Department, [city officials] point to the record and say they have a minimal number of complaints," Cofield said. "The problem is the data does not support much of the perception. And we believe that people have been so intimidated that they have not filed formal complaints.

"As I expressed to the police chief, we have some people who have come forward and indicated that they had gone to speak to police officers, and that they had been so grilled and so questioned that they were literally intimidated into not filing formal complaints," said Cofield. "One of the commitments we want to make to citizens of Harris County is that we will contact necessary authorities and walk with them through that process."

The NAACP also called for complaints to be reviewed by an outside party to help determine if the department has a problem.

"You do not allow students to grade their own papers," Cofield said. "Inevitably they will grade themselves much higher than they deserve."

It was only through the pressure of the NAACP that the City of Bellaire agreed to set up a police complaint center and a 1-800 number for complaints. According to the *Houston Chronicle*, the Bellaire Assistant City Manager Diane K. White said the process was a "positive step" in addressing the allegations of racial profiling.

"The City of Bellaire and the Bellaire Police Department take the allegations of racial profiling that have surfaced very seriously," White said.

Call me cynical, but as far as I could see, the City of Bellaire didn't really take the allegations that seriously, at least when it came to changing the very structure of the police department. According to the *Houston Chronicle*, the Bellaire Police Department had forty-one members, with thirteen Hispanic officers and only two black ones. All the other officers were white, and the city and police department weren't even addressing that.

In 2007, when the department was accused of two incidents

of racial profiling, the Bellaire Police Department immediately discounted these complaints as not credible. In my case, the Bellaire Police Department didn't focus on how it had wronged me or what it could do to make my life better, but instead, it praised Sgt. Cotton, talking about how, despite damn near killing me, the officer was a so-called excellent ten-year veteran of the force.

I don't think that I'm being overly sensitive when I say that as a resident of Bellaire, the city's main concern should have been to make sure that my welfare was the prime focus of everyone in government. Call me naïve, but I expected a statement from the city and the police department that sounded something like this:

"We find the shooting of Robbie Tolan, a young man who'd done nothing wrong, to be an abomination. It was a complete breakdown in our procedure, and we can't allow our residents to believe that they are at risk with people who are sworn to protect and serve the community. The police officers that were involved in this unfortunate incident were immediately fired, and we're opening discussions with the family to make them whole. We apologize to the Tolans, and we hope that they know that we feel that they are valued members of the community who should be shown respect."

However that didn't happen, and I could see what was about to occur. If the City of Bellaire and its police department had anything to do with it, I was going to be a forgotten footnote in the city I grew up in. They wanted to erase me.

Surprisingly, there weren't that many protest marches for me, despite the fact that in Houston we'd had many marches for black non-Houstonian victims of police violence like Trayvon Martin, Michael Brown, and Sandra Bland. Granted, these black people had been killed and that heightened the passions around their cases of police brutality, but even though I'd survived, I still needed that support. But the people didn't come out for me like they did for others. I think the mindset was, "Yeah, what happened to you sucked, but you're alive, so get over it. The others are dead. We're speaking for them."

Unexpectedly, the press did a pretty good job at highlighting the issue of me being shot by the police and the issue of racial profiling. The *Houston Press* did a satirical piece called "It's Easier Than You Think to Get Shot by a Bellaire Cop," in which they pointed out five different absurd ways you could get shot, including "Drive a 2004 Nissan Xterra," because "it's only natural that brazenly driving around in one of these house-parties-in-an-SUV would get you labeled a car thief," and my favorite, "Stick up for Mom," because "when the officer roughly grabs your mother and slams her against the garage door, any movement at all on your part will of course be interpreted as an attempt to steal the officer's weapon and use it on him. Congratulations! Enjoy your bullet wound."

My dad did tell me that there was support for me online. He brought me a laptop so I could go to various news websites, which is something in retrospect I don't particularly advise.

If you ever want to see yourself reduced to a racist stereotype, where your black skin is used in any and every possible way to dehumanize you, then my advice is to get shot by a white police officer and watch the reactions from people that post in the comments section. Yeah, I know that you're not supposed to read the ranting of people who hide behind their anonymity, but I think it's a human reaction to want to have other humans empathize, or at least sympathize, with your plight. Let me just say that it didn't quite turn out that way for me.

Some were like, "This really sucks that this happened," which you'd think is the bare minimum metric for getting a compassionate human reaction. Other comments basically said, "He got what he deserved," or even more strangely, "He's some rich kid," as though your bank account determined whether or not the bullet you took was justified. Honestly, cooped up in that hospital, all I wanted to feel was some support as a way to connect with people, but when I read the comments, they only discouraged me. I hate having to admit that, but yeah, reading comments that had no sympathy was a real downer. However, a few weeks later, I taped an interview with HBO's *Real Sports with Bryant Gumbel*, and that's when things began to change.

"Why would Bryant Gumbel want to talk to me?" I asked when I was told that he was on the phone. I soon found the answer.

"I'm really pissed off by this," Gumbel told me when I got on the phone. There wasn't a lot of small talk because my lungs weren't strong enough for me to talk for long, so Gumbel did most of the talking. "I want to feature you on my show."

Gumbel was the first person who wasn't a family member to really understand the bigger picture and empathize with what I'd gone through. When we talked, I could tell that he related to the fear of having a loved one be at the mercy of the police, simply because their blackness was thought to present a clear danger to the white cop in front of them.

He talked about how his son, Bradley Gumbel, had been harassed and roughed up by the cops. Bradley, who stands over six feet four inches, had been told that he looked suspicious and was taken to jail. Gumbel had said that the only thing that had saved Bradley from the fate that had doomed the Sandra Blands of the world was the fact that he had resources to get his son out of jail quickly.

So I appeared on *Real Sports with Bryant Gumbel* for a segment called *Black in Bellaire*. The problem? I had to go back to the Woodstock house, the scene of my shooting, to tape the segment. Obviously, I wasn't thrilled about that. David Scott, Bryant's producer, informed me that they wanted to get shots of me on the way to the house and arriving at the house in order to give the audience an idea of what happened. David and Bryant were both very respectful of our wishes and emotions, but I also knew that if my story was going to have any impact, unfortunately I was going to have to re-enact what happened in Bellaire as accurately as possible.

As we drove to Woodstock, I could feel myself getting more and more anxious, and as we turned onto our street, my heart began pounding. I looked up at what used to be my home to see my parents, Bryant, and three other cameramen standing outside. It was surreal. What the hell was I thinking when I agreed to do this?

I'm not sure if my reaction would have been the same had there been no cameras, but I was almost emotionless. From the moment I stepped out of the car, my first moments back at the house were all recorded on tape. There were no cuts. Every raw second was captured. Bryant introduced himself to me as we walked up the driveway toward the house, and I was thinking we would begin the interview inside, but he started asking me questions, on camera, before I even made it onto the porch.

Inside the house, our living room had been transformed into

a studio, with all of the furniture removed and a black drape covering everything. That actually helped, because I didn't want to be reminded of the house I grew up in that was now sullied by this incident.

We ate lunch before the interview, and since I was just getting back my appetite, it was cool to just be able to sit down, eat, and chat with Gumbel, who I'd only seen on TV for most all of my life. I think the impression people often get of Gumbel is that he's a bit aloof and distant, but I can say after having met him that they couldn't be more wrong. Gumbel was not only warm and friendly, but he also cursed like a sailor, which definitely endeared him to me! We laughed and made jokes, and by the time I sat down for the interview, I was somewhat comfortable enough to talk.

You'd think that with all of my trepidation about coming back to the scene of my shooting I'd be scared of talking about the details of getting shot by Sgt. Cotton, but you know, I wasn't. When you're speaking the truth, you really have nothing to be nervous about. There's nothing you have to hide or think twice about. Just tell your story and be your authentic self. My feeling is that the story will resonate with people who see you for who you truly are and not the two-dimensional media caricature or racial stereotype they want you to be.

Even though I'd cried plenty of tears over the physical and emotional pain I'd suffered, I was determined to not cry my way into the hearts of the viewers. I had to dig deep, but I wanted them to see my strength, how I hadn't allowed this devastating setback to break me. That has been my attitude throughout this incident. Don't let them see your weaknesses and vulnerabilities.

In a curious way, I wanted to be a symbol of inspiration and motivation, one others could turn to when they went through their own challenges. Everyone was surprised that I interviewed so well, except of course my mom, who thinks her beloved son does everything well. But there was one question that Bryant asked that hit me hard.

"What part of you feels like 'my ship has sailed'?"

"The part of me that has the bullet in it."

My answer went deeper than I had anticipated. Many people thought that I was talking about my baseball career. They were wrong. I was being literal. I wanted to make sure that people knew that even though the bullet had done a lot of damage to my body, it was still just a tiny part of who I was. It occupied just a few inches of my being, and the rest of my body was more than ready to get back to being what it could be, whether that was living up to my potential as a baseball player or just a regular human being. I wouldn't deny that the bullet was part of me, but I refused to make it all of me.

After the show aired, the comments began to change. Before, I was just a news report on the local news or a story in the newspaper. But after I was on *Real Sports,* most people saw me as a human being.

I received hundreds of emails from people around the world saying that they couldn't believe what had happened. I remember one letter from a woman in Holland who talked about how she couldn't believe that America could allow this to happen to its citizens. Another woman, an American, talked about being in an interracial marriage and having to watch her black husband be harassed by the police. The public was starting to empathize and sympathize with me. I was relatable.

I didn't become a national symbol for police violence like many other black people who had died at the hands of police officers. There weren't any hashtag campaigns on my behalf, but I did feel the support. People were calling me a hero, and I couldn't really understand that. I didn't cure cancer; I didn't run into a burning building to save an elderly person. I was only trying to protect my mom from being roughed up. So I didn't feel like a hero; I just felt like everyone would have done the same thing.

I've learned over the years that there's something in America's DNA that only allows us to be shocked by racism and the violence that comes with it if we have some type of personal connection. Black and Latino people live with racism on a day-to-day basis, but white Americans always appear to be shocked every time racism rears its ugly head. I find it to be damn scary that I've gotta rely on your personal experience with racism for you to care. I'm pretty sure it's the same way with sexism, where if the victim of sexism looks like a wife, girlfriend, sister, or mother, then we have empathy, but if it's some random woman we don't know or a systemic issue with misogyny, then we tend to be dispassionate.

In some ways, that's sad, mainly because I don't want to walk this earth as a black man who depends on people having a relationship with some other black men before they can overcome their prejudices and empathize with me when something bad happens. The comments sections of the news sites showed me that many white people don't have that empathy, and as a result, my getting shot is seen as an "oh well" in their lives. I mean nothing to them. And when you're seen as nothing, you get death threats designed to let you know that you're nothing.

"I thought America would be smart enough not to elect some Arab as president. But now ignorant niggers like you and your family want to cry wolf and try to make a buck off good wholesome, hard working Americans. I didn't think welfare paid out enough to move into Bellaire. You people should have been happy they even let you in Bellaire. I agree that the shooting of you in front of your house was tragic. It was tragic that the cop only shot you once. You're lucky I wasn't there. I would have stood over you and looked you in the eye. I would have loved to see the expression on your face with a pistol pressed up against your forehead before I pulled the trigger...."

After the *Real Sports with Bryant Gumbel* interview, my mother went to the back room and brought out a trash bag full of letters that had been sent to me. I read some; some were supportive, others not so much, but it was this one that stuck out.

"I swear to God I'm going to finish what Sergeant Cotton started. And I'm a former cop, I know how to get away with it. Just like Sergeant Cotton will. Every time I see your fucking mug on the TV I get so angry. I want to drive over to your house and blow it to the sky. Don't worry, Mr. Tolan, you'll be seeing me at the trial, if you even make it that long. You'll recognize me, I'll be the last one you see before you die!!!"

Many people told me that I should ignore the ignorant people who wrote letters like this and that I should just concentrate on the positive people who backed my new struggle. That's easy to say when it isn't you in the crosshairs, metaphorically or literally. But forget about the death threat; there was something else the author of this letter wrote that struck me to the core.

He'd be seeing me at the trial.

No, I wasn't worried that this nutcase was gonna show up at the trial. I was worried about something a bit more ominous. Even if we could get the district attorney to bring charges on Sgt. Cotton, which would be extremely difficult mainly because the American public and the criminal justice system give wide latitude to law enforcement to use their own judgment in using force, I'd still have to deal with a jury consisting of my Bellaire peers, and Sgt. Cotton only needed *one* Mr. Death Threat on the jury to win. In order for me to ultimately win justice, my case depended on the ability of a dozen people, probably mostly white, to have some sort of empathy toward me; this would require them to both see my race as it relates to why I was shot, which was the racial profiling aspect, and look past my race and the racial stereotypes they may hold.

A documentary on race that was created about twenty or thirty years ago, called *Ethnic Notions,* did a magnificent job describing how America created the various stereotypes about black people being ignorant, violent, or nonhuman. It talked about how black men in particular were seen as black brutes and about the horrible stereotypes of black men being animalistic with only violence on their minds and, as a result, needing white authority figures like cops to keep them in line. White Americans grow up, whether they know it or not, believing this. So when a person like me gets shot, the immediate reaction is to consciously and unconsciously default back to those stereotypes. How do you get justice with those stereotypes engrained in the brains of predominately white juries?

It was going to be a huge task, and the task was made harder by the toll it was taking on my family. Just a week after I was shot, my father ended up in St. Luke's Hospital, the same place where I'd been transferred earlier, because he had to have an emergency double bypass heart surgery. There was so much family visiting both of us that St. Luke's moved me to the heart unit so that relatives could visit us together. So there we were at St. Luke's Hospital together on the same floor, fighting for our lives.

My mom and dad insisted that my dad's surgery didn't have anything to do with my situation, but let's be real. The stress of watching your son get shot and nearly killed surely didn't help. The stress tried to kill him, and this crushed me. I'm the young one, the son who's supposed to help his parents stay strong as they grow older, but at least in my brain, I was now the cause of them becoming weaker.

Then again, I'm not much different than my dad. In my hospital room, I didn't want to hear about anything to do with my shooting. I wanted to be joyful and positive, and anything that kept my mind off being in a hospital room was a welcome distraction. Anything else was a negative. It was then that I started to have my first psychological issues around that negativity.

You can call it what you want—survivor's remorse, survivor's guilt, or just plain fucked up in the head—but all of the negativity I'd been trying to keep away from me began to flood my brain just weeks after having been shot. It was as though the negative thoughts had been building up behind a mud dam, and when the dam ultimately broke, my brain was trying to hold back the Nile River. I started having nightmares about being shot, waking up in the middle of the night, sweating through my sheets.

In baseball, your mental strength is key. You're nothing without it. After all, baseball is a game where if you fail seven out of ten times at the plate, and do it long enough, you're paid millions and make the Hall of Fame. To succeed at baseball, you have to be mentally tough enough to not only shrug off failure after failure, but also somehow figure out how to succeed at hitting a baseball traveling at close to one hundred miles per hour day after day.

However, getting shot isn't like playing a game. A pitcher throwing a ball at my head could theoretically kill me, but at least I know that he's not trying to kill me. A police officer shooting me *is* trying to kill me. Guns and bullets are designed to kill, and psychologically, I couldn't get over the fact that I'd been targeted for death, and it was only by sheer fate that I'd survived, unlike the two other black men who'd died in the same twenty-four hours that New Year's holiday.

That's why I couldn't go back to live at my parents' house on Woodstock when I got out of the hospital. I just couldn't do it. I tried to tell myself that the house had nothing to do with me being shot, but the closer I got to being released from St. Luke's, the more terrified I became of having to relive the shooting every time I wanted to go to the store, walk around the block, or just sleep.

Yes, I was deathly tired of being in the hospital. I wanted to end the poking, the prodding, the painful, well, everything that was associated with being shot. However, at the same time, the hospital was my safe space. I was anonymous, a private person living in a private room, and no one could find me. No one could harm me, either for real or with their cruel words. I was a man without a place in the world. I was Unknown 90, safe in the anonymity that the doctors and staff had created for me. It was a bubble—an artificial bubble, but a safe bubble nonetheless. And then it went away.

"The doctors said you may be able to be released in the next day or so," my mom said. I just nodded impassively.

"That doesn't make you happy?"

"I don't have anywhere to go," I said. "And I don't wanna go home."

I felt like a man who'd almost drowned and was now being taken back to the same pool. Maybe I'd watched too many bad gangster movies, but I had this weird feeling that the Bellaire police would come back and try to finish the job if I stayed there. Irrational? Maybe. But getting shot for driving your own car is irrational. Whatever. All I knew is that I didn't want to live on Woodstock anymore. It just wasn't home anymore. I didn't want anything to do with the City of Bellaire. I didn't want to have anything do with that house, and in fact, I wanted my parents to get rid of it as soon as it happened.

I wanted my parents to leave, but the reality was that this had been their home for fifteen years. We weren't ballers who could just up and leave because we wanted to. In a perfect world, none of us would have returned, but we're regular human beings, with debts and bills, and despite the bad memories now associated with the shooting, the reality was that my parents had to stay there.

But I didn't. I had a choice. I was going to stay at my Aunt Carolyn's.

"You happy to be out of that hospital I bet, aren't you?" said Aunt Carolyn, as we pulled out of St. Luke's Hospital. I nodded my head.

"I never thought I'd be outside alive again."

I stuck my head slightly outside of the window like a dog. For the first time in my life, I was amazed by and appreciative of all the simple things we take for granted every day.

As Aunt Carolyn drove, I closed my eyes and smiled as the sun hit me in the face. I watched the wind push my hand back and giggled like a child, rediscovering something I had been deprived of and thought I'd never see again. I don't think I put my head back inside the car until we got to Aunt Carolyn's house in nearby Missouri City.

If I was going to have deal with demons, at least I wasn't going to live where the demons had come into my life. Woodstock was forever dead to me. There was no peace or love there anymore.

## CHAPTER 3

# THE JOURNEY FOR JUSTICE BEGINS

**Tarika Wilson, 26, Lima, Ohio—January 4, 2008**

During a drug raid targeting her boyfriend, twenty-six-year-old Tarika Wilson, an African American woman, was shot and killed by Sergeant Joseph Chavalia. The unarmed mother of six children was shot while hiding behind a bedroom door, as was her one-year-old son, Sincere Wilson, who lost a finger. According to the American Civil Liberties Union, another officer shot Wilson's two dogs, which caused Sgt. Chavalia to believe that gunfire was coming from inside the apartment. Sgt. Chavalia shot through the door without identifying himself. An all-white jury acquitted Sgt. Chavalia of negligent homicide and negligent assault.

et me first say that there's no checklist or some *Getting Shot by the Police for Dummies* book to help someone mentally deal with the aftermath of police violence. And that's a damn shame because life comes at you fast when you are the victim of police violence. Just one day after my surgery, it became quite apparent that we were going to need some help. Media requests were coming in left and right; the police wanted statements from us, as though they were trying to prove that we were really criminals, but they just hadn't figured out how; and we needed to know our rights. No one in my family was a lawyer, but I knew that we needed to sue these bastards for what they did to me.

My Aunt Tammy, my mother's sister, worked as a paralegal at a law firm, so she was way ahead of us. We relied on her to get us legal representation, and she started calling potential lawyers when I first got to the hospital. That's how I got to my first set of lawyers: David Berg, George Gibson, and David's son, Geoffrey Berg.

When we first met with David and Geoff in my hospital room, it was weird. Can you be both confident and pessimistic at the same time? If so, our lawyers were just that. Initially, my family fell in love with them because they seemed to be just what you wanted in lawyers: witty, smart, and charismatic. Did you have questions about the process? No problem. Geoff made himself available to anyone who had questions, and he was at the hospital constantly, checking on me and then going to the conference room to check on my relatives. We were neophytes at this, and they were the pros, and we soon had a comfort level with them that felt like we'd be okay in their hands. But there were issues with how they saw our case versus how we saw our case.

On the one hand, they were really confident about our civil case, saying that they'd never had a case with this much evidence against a police officer. We got the vibe that they felt this was a no-brainer, an open and shut win against Cotton, the City of Bellaire, and the Bellaire Police Department. We were in the right; they were in the wrong, so that made us confident. On the other hand, however, they were pessimistic about getting an indictment in the criminal case. Geoff, who was acting as our spokesperson, really didn't think it was going to happen. And what he told us privately was a tad bit different than the face he presented publicly.

"This is Texas. Very Republican. Everyone is a straight shooter," I recall him saying. "And at the end of the day, it all boils down to a white cop shooting a black kid." I remember he talked about how the cops, the district attorney (DA), and all of the judges were buddies, which meant that we didn't have a chance to even get to first base, which was the criminal indictment. So, ultimately, he was convinced that the criminal case was hopeless.

"I'm not trying to get your hopes up, and I want you to be realistic," he told us, "and I'm not going to sugarcoat this for you, but I'm not optimistic about getting an indictment for this criminal case."

But our hands were tied until the criminal case was done. There could be no civil case until the criminal case was handled. So we had to wait to see whether the Harris County District Attorney's Office would indict Sgt. Cotton for shooting me. For the public, Geoff had to at least create the charade that we had a chance for an indictment.

"He [Sgt. Cotton] will now be afforded the presumption of innocence that he did not provide Robbie Tolan and the Tolan family on December 31st of last year," said Geoffrey Berg to the press. "We are going to assist the district attorney in any way we can and whatever way they request."

Even though people say that a DA can get any grand jury to indict a ham sandwich, we all know that indicting police officers in the killing or shooting of black people is damn near impossible, whether you're in conservative Texas or liberal Massachusetts. And the studies bare this out.

Bowling Green State University professor Philip Matthew Stinson, who is one of the country's leading researchers on the subject, studied over ten thousand police arrests for misconduct and concluded that only if an officer did something really egregious, such as running a criminal drug ring or murdering someone while engaged in criminal behavior, then, yeah, a grand jury was down for indicting the officer. The cop had to be dirty in order for him or her to be judged as a criminal. But what about situations like mine, where a police officer was supposedly making a split-second decision about either his life or mine? Indictments are much rarer in these cases.

According to Professor Stinson, there are between nine hundred and a thousand shootings per year during which an on-duty cop fatally shoots someone. Less than 2 percent of these officers are charged with murder or manslaughter. And even when the 36 percent of charged officers are convicted, they're usually convicted on a lesser charge. In other words, something less than murder or attempted murder, like aggravated assault, was the only way to get an indictment.

"If the jury is sitting there thinking, 'Oh my God. A split-second decision like that? What would I have done? Would I have shot the guy?' you're not going to get an indictment," Professor Stinson said.

That's not a very good thing to read when you realize that your particular case fits this scenario. So we didn't have our hopes up when it came to getting a criminal indictment from the Harris County District Attorney's Office. An investigator named Keith Webb, from the Police Integrity Division in the District Attorney's Office, interviewed us to determine whether the officers used proper procedure during the incident, but Geoff Berg still remained skeptical.

Part of the reason why Geoff was skeptical is because prosecutors control the grand jury proceedings, which means they can present as much or as little information as they think prudent. They can leave out evidence if they want, or they can favor one side over the other in order to persuade the grand jury to see the case in a way that suits them. Prosecutors work with police on a regular basis, and most don't like damaging their relationships by indicting police officers. This is just a fact.

We all did deposition with the Harris County DAs, first my mom and dad, and then Anthony, but to be honest, I just thought it was all a dog and pony show. And then they got to me.

Two men from the DA's office set up video cameras around Aunt Carolyn's dining room table and then spread out dozens of diagrams, pictures, and anything else that was connected to the crime scene. And when I say crime scene, I'm pointing to what I think was Sgt. Cotton's shooting of me, and not anything that I did to make it happen.

My lawyer, Geoff Berg, sat to my left as they questioned me, while my family was in the next room holding a prayer vigil for me. I didn't get the feeling that the DA's office was trying to bait me into saying something untrue, but we spent hours going over everything in minute detail. Since I'd been told by Geoff that it was nearly impossible to get a criminal indictment, I thought these depositions were designed to make the public feel like justice was there for everyone and that they'd hold Sgt. Cotton to the highest standards, but in the end, this wouldn't really be the case. They'd hold a public press conference where they'd lament the fact that the grand jury hadn't returned an indictment, but they would maintain they had done all of their due diligence. To be completely fair, I do have to say that they were very thorough.

I drew on diagrams, explained details, and then drew on even more diagrams. To the best of my recollection, I explained what I could explain. By the way, trying to have a broader perspective of a traumatic event you're trying to forget is not an easy thing. I constantly questioned whether things happened the way I thought they did, knowing that a simply mistake, or as politicians like to say, "misremembering," could torpedo my case in the eyes of the DA's office or make it vulnerable to a defense attorney poring over my deposition for any inconsistency that would lead to a shadow of a doubt acquittal. But for the most part, I think things went well, and after about two hours, just like that, the DAs were gone.

Then, about a week or two later, came the thunderbolt.

"Um, the DA just indicted Jeffrey Cotton," Berg said. It was early in the morning, and strangely, Berg didn't sound excited, but kind of pensive, almost dumbfounded. It was like he was amazed that it had happened or like he didn't believe in a million years that he'd be saying those words. That may have been the first time I experienced real doubt that Berg and the rest of his crew were the lawyers we needed for the long haul, because when it came to my family's response to the news, we weren't surprised in the least.

We Tolans believe in prayer, so all this time we had faith in Jesus that since we were in the right, an indictment was definitely in the offing, just as long as we kept praying. I had no misgivings. We were going to get that indictment, and sure enough, Cotton was indicted for aggravated assault.

Maybe I should talk about how my family relied not just on the criminal justice system, but also on our faith, because sometimes prayer gets relegated to the sidelines in incidents like this. There's an old cliché that says there are no atheists in war, and I'd say the same thing about getting shot by the police. My family's faith in God strengthened as our trials and tribulations deepened. That shouldn't be a surprise to anyone.

Getting shot by the police is like falling into an abyss of darkness, with no road map as to how to get to the light. But my faith in Jesus helped me believe that there was a light, even when pessimism and depression conspired to work against my family and me. So no, we weren't surprised that we'd gotten that indictment. After all, what is faith but believing even when the evidence tells you to stop believing?

As for my attorneys, no matter how much they said they cared about the case or how much we liked their demeanor with us, it's important to remember that, at the end of the day, I was just another client for them. Yes, they may have been passionate about seeking justice, and hey, that's why we hired them, but, as lawyers, their main goal was to get the monetary reward that comes from fighting a case and, if fortunate, winning the case. I'm not trying to be cynical or pessimistic, but their interest was the civil case, and they never expected the criminal case to go anywhere. For them, of course, it wasn't a matter of faith, but of pragmatism. Yeah, they were probably pleased, if not a bit shocked, by the unexpected indictment. But at the end of the day, all that mattered to them was the civil case. As for me, a fight to the end was the only option, so I cared about the criminal case as much as the civil one. My family wanted justice in both cases.

"The district clerk will receive the indictment in this case. At that time, a cause number and a felony district court will be assigned. Prosecutors from our district attorney's Police Integrity Division will handle this case through its disposition," said Harris County Assistant District Attorney Donna Hawkins.

We actually got a grand jury to treat us better than that ham sandwich. Black men don't often get that type of treatment when they're up against police officers. As for the City of Bellaire and their reaction, well they were still in a fantasyland about how and why my shooting had happened. We knew that I'd been shot because I was black, but the Bellaire city manager, Bernie Satterwhite, as usual, denied that race had anything to do with the bullet in my body.

"Neither any action nor statement by the grand jury or the district attorney's office has suggested, and the city has not learned of any evidence, indicating that the city's policies or lack of training played any role in the incident. All Bellaire police officers, including Sgt. Cotton, are trained and certified in accordance with Texas-mandated initial and continuing training requirements. There is nothing about the indictment or any investigation which even suggests that race played any role in the stop or Sgt. Cotton's actions when he arrived as a back-up officer."

You know, I honestly didn't care what he had to say. I knew what was up, and three months after having been shot, this was one of the first positive signs that I just might get some justice. But our lawyers hit back hard in a statement in response to the city's.

"I think there's a tremendous contrast between what happened in Dallas recently and what happened in Bellaire," Geoffrey Berg said, referring to a police shooting that had recently occurred. "The chief of the Dallas Police Department came out immediately and said he was sorry for what had happened and that was for an egregious situation in which a young man was prevented from being by his mother-in-law's bedside as she lay dying. Robbie Tolan was shot. And we still have no apology, so there is a great deal the Bellaire Police Department could do."

In my heart of hearts, I think the appearance on *Real Sports* had something to do with the indictment. It put me in the national spotlight, and it took the bandage off the rotten situation that was happening in Bellaire. If my shooting had only garnered local attention, I think they would have buried and ignored it. But now, it was getting national, even worldwide attention.

For my mom, the indictment proved to be the spur for trying to get me justice. Her crusade became borderline obsessive, and you could tell that she felt this was her calling. She was a woman who'd already gone through so much in her life.

Before having me, my mother had three miscarriages, and so she knew the devastating effect of personal loss and the ache that never goes away. I can't imagine what it's like to nurture a life inside you and then have it die through no fault of your own. Life itself became more precious to her because she didn't take it for granted. But she was also having her faith tested. She and my father were almost coming to grips with the fact that it appeared that God didn't have it in His plans for them to have a child.

Then my mother became pregnant with me, and it seemed like the same cycle would happen yet again. She was pregnant with two babies, twins, and my twin had died. As for me, the doctor told her that it didn't look good because all of my vital signs appeared weak.

But the doctor said a curious thing, something that went beyond the medical training.

"I've had success with this, and it might sound crazy," the doctor told her, "but if you talk to your baby like he's born, the positivity might just help him be okay."

So my mom tried to channel all of her positive feelings into this little baby boy who wasn't supposed to be born. In order to not jinx it, she didn't even tell my dad until the last minute that she was pregnant. It was just me and her.

"Come on baby," she would whisper to me while rubbing her pregnant belly. "It's just you and me. I can't wait to meet you, and I promise that I will love and protect you for all of your life."

And three decades later, here I am. So if you think that she was going to let a police officer try to kill her miracle baby and get away with it, you don't know Marian Tolan very well. And I love her for it. I owe her for my life, and I'd happily give it to make sure that she stays safe in this world.

My mom has always been the rock of the family. Why? Because she just knows how to run shit. Point blank. When people don't know what to do in a situation, they call my mom. She's always on it and takes care of business. My mom is the first person people call when they need to get something done or fixed, and if they're almost done with something, she's also the last person they call to see if they've done things right.

And I needed that. I needed a fierce advocate who wouldn't blink or crumble under pressure—someone who I thought could be vocal for me when I wanted to retreat into silence and anonymity. My mom fit the bill to the tee.

My dad's nature is a bit passive when it comes to overtly fighting, but don't get me wrong, he's a fighter, just not in the same way as my mom. However, my dad has never been one to openly express his feelings. He'd come to the hospital, ask me how I was doing, and then not say much else. My dad came from an earlier age that taught men to remain emotionless about the devastating impact of tragedy on their lives, but if you scratched just below the surface, you'd see that he was just as disgusted as everyone else. He felt the pain that comes with seeing your child hurting. I felt my dad's presence, and I could also feel how he was trying to bear the weight of the family, and it was literally tearing him up inside.

Me? As the victim in this saga, there were times when I wanted to fight and then other times when it was so overwhelming that I just wanted to crawl into a hole. Whether or not I felt like fighting depended on my mood for the day. But my mom? She never wavered. I never saw her tire of fighting. And the one thing she was very adamant about was not settling. There would never be any talk about settling from the lawyers.

"These people are not going to continue to throw hush money at people and think that they can get away with it," she told the lawyers. "That's not an option." My mom wanted our story to be heard, and she wanted the underbelly of police violence against black people to be shown. Unfortunately, that would be a bone of contention with us as the court cases got to the end point.

Part of that showing the true face of Bellaire was keeping our story in the media. I was very selective about who I talked to about the shooting, mainly because it took a mental toll on me each time I had to relive it, even though I was prepared.

Remember when I said that I was a weird little kid and that I had practiced giving interviews as a child? I would give myself these interviews after baseball games. I would pay attention to reporters on TV and see how they conducted interviews. I grew up around big baseball stars like Ken Griffey Jr. and Tony Gwynn, so I got to see them in their element, giving press conferences and clubhouse interviews, and then in their home life. I got to see how they conducted themselves both on and off the field, and so I tried to mimic that. After all, I thought that I was going to be a famous baseball player when I grew up.

When I was shot, and I had to do press conferences and interviews, it felt like I'd been preparing for this my whole life. I wasn't caught off guard by anything, and I didn't suddenly turn timid when speaking to the media. I was very poised, and this was me finally in the game shooting free throws after I'd practiced all night. I wasn't scared.

But I knew that I even if I was poised, I still needed to think about my point of view on the shooting and how people would interpret my answers. Every time I was in the media, I tried to think about each and every question a reporter would ask me so that I was prepared. It wasn't like they were trying to trick me, but I did know that each reporter had the power and ability to shape the narrative about me. If someone doesn't know me or comes to the interview with thoughts about black men and the police that contradict my own real story, then there's a real possibility that the person will skew my story. You can't come back from that. But by preparing so thoroughly, I was able to maintain a sense of control that, even if it was illusionary, was just enough to keep me sane. I made sure to keep any impulse responses, you know, like being the stereotype of the angry black man, out of the public eye, and my frustrations were only meted out in privacy.

Nonetheless, I felt that I was under a microscope and

constrained in a box shaped by American society. I couldn't take ownership of the rational angry feelings I had for being wronged because I know that America won't allow a black man to be angry around issues of race. Maybe it was the stoic face of Martin Luther King, Jr. and his nonviolent movement or something else that was burned into the psyche of our American id, but at no point did I feel like my true angry self could be the face I showed the media. It wouldn't have helped my cause at all.

I knew that I had to carry myself differently than some white guy in the same position, mainly because I'd watched my cousin Ken Griffey Jr. and our good friend Tony Gwynn, both of whom were my childhood heroes, act the same way. I watched their faces when a reporter would ask, "How are you feeling after that loss?" And you could see that they wanted to say, "What type of stupid ass question is that?" But they never did. They weren't allowed to be angry black baseball players, and yet they kept their humanity as they talked about their frustrations, always with class. I knew that I had to carry myself with that same class.

To be fair, most of the Houston media was very nice to me. I didn't feel any type of malice from them, nor did they take advantage of the situation or take advantage of me. Their questions were fair, and most were interested in going beyond the whole "black man shot by white police officer" narrative and wanted to see the humanity in me. And for the most part, they were able to do that. We got some really great stories about black people in Bellaire from the *Houston Chronicle*, and it exposed the racism white residents had ignored or didn't know about in the first place. However, I still only did the occasional interview. My mom? She had a different strategy.

My mom believed that, in order to make sure that people didn't forget me or just reduce me to a statistic or a social media hashtag, she had to talk to everyone. It didn't matter if it was *The New York Times* or the *June Bug Backyard* newspaper, if she could tell my story, she'd tell my story. We bumped heads about this because I wanted to pick my interviews wisely and the lawyers weren't sure that she should be out there talking about the case. But thank God that she did, because I didn't have the energy or willpower to do it. On the other hand, this did expose her to a backlash from people who didn't think I had a legitimate reason to be declared a victim of police violence.

I remember when she appeared on one local Houston radio show very early on and she was talking about her passion for the fight, along with the broader problem of police violence against black men. My mom was new at this and still trying to find her voice, but she talked about how we needed support from the community when it came to police brutality against black people and how nine times out of ten the victims died during these confrontations, so she looked at my case as a unique opportunity to speak for those who couldn't speak for themselves. Sounds pretty reasonable, right? Well the radio host, a guy named Michael Harris who has one of the oldest black radio shows in Houston, basically told her that she should keep quiet and just be grateful that I hadn't died.

His premise was that only the black mothers who'd lost their children to police violence had a real reason to complain and that, because these mothers would give their right arms to get their kids back, my mom had no right to complain. You are over here complaining about the criminal justice system, but you should really just go home and hug your son and be glad that he's still here was the essence of his statements. I was infuriated after I heard that interview, thinking to myself, "What an idiot!"

However, if I am to be completely honest, my mom's dogged advocacy for me did produce a bit of a rift between us. No matter how much a person loves you, cares about you, and wants to do right by you, the pain you feel from being shot is still theoretical to them. They can sympathize and be outraged for you, but they're not going through it physically and mentally as you are. At times, I think my mom didn't understand that her crusade to see me get justice was also taking a toll on me, day to day, month to month, year to year.

Yes, my goal was justice, but it also was to get back to being a normal human being, and that's not something you should take lightly. You don't miss being normal until your life is abnormal, just like you don't appreciate walking until you're disabled. To be who I was before I was shot was my strongest drive and my biggest priority. So practically, there were times when I didn't have the strength to concentrate on the details of the case or what was happening with other black police shooting victims, because I was concentrating on how to sleep through the night without pain or on one of a hundred other things on my list of obstacles to overcome that were hidden from the public and my family. I think my mom took me not concentrating exclusively on the fight as me losing my spirit, or at least not being as determined as she was. But that wasn't the case.

No one wants to be a victim, but I learned a few things about being one. Being a victim is a balance between wanting your victimhood avenged, or at least somehow acknowledged by the people, group, or entity that wronged you, while at the same time, not letting yourself be consumed by that victimhood. Other people have a hard time understanding how you couldn't be consumed by victimhood because, as they try to empathize, they think to themselves about what *they'd* do in your place. That was my mom's position, and add to that the fact that she gives me unconditional love, and you have the passionate fighter I talked about earlier. And that's great. But as much as my mom loves me, she isn't me and this wasn't her life. Yet she seemed consumed by telling me about what I needed to do to keep the fight going, and you can't fault me for having rebelled from time to time, as the last thing I wanted was to have someone else control my life at a time when I felt like it was so out of control. Our relationship suffered in some ways during this period, but later, it would strengthen.

While I tried to navigate between balancing my need for self-care and fighting a system, the one thing I learned that was completely out of my control was the criminal justice system and whether or not justice would prevail. The indictment was announced in April of 2009, and the trial occurred in May of 2010. However, the trial was rescheduled three times, which really made me feel like the criminal justice system was fucking with me. I now know that trials get rescheduled all of the time as a result of scheduling conflicts, but as a lay person who'd never dealt with lawyers or trials, it felt like I was the last thing on their mind, like they were never going to have the trial.

I felt like the criminal justice element was a great labyrinth where not only justice is blind, but you are too. I don't know if they make the rules and procedures intentionally complicated so that you're reliant on lawyers and judges, but that's how it felt. No matter how many explanations we got from Berg or the Harris County DA, it always felt like we were in the dark.

On the other hand, the rest of my life was starting to make sense again. I spent the year prior to the criminal trial in constant rehab, at first just trying to get back to feeling like a normal human being who could walk without feeling like I was going to faint from exhaustion. I eventually got to the point where I felt like I was on the brink of being an athlete again. The hospital sent over a nurse to my Aunt Carolyn's to check my vitals, but for the most part, getting healed and healthy was all on me.

You often hear professional athletes talk about rehab being a lonely process, not only because they are hurt but also because they feel disconnected and isolated. This isolation comes in a number of ways.

You're disconnected from family and friends who tend to approach each day without having to deal with limitations, so they have a limited understanding of what you're going through. Even if you're permanently disabled physically, you're still able to create a world of normal limitations that you're used to. If your life confines you to a wheelchair, then you know what you can and can't do while in that wheelchair. For me, I had to sweat, cry, and struggle through the frustration of knowing that my physical wholeness was just over the horizon, but I'd first need to climb out of a hole that seemed impossible to climb out of. And yet I knew that I had to do it. Every step out of that hole was a victory against the City of Bellaire and the Bellaire Police Department.

You're disconnected from the things you love when you're in rehab. It may sound funny, but I wanted to get back to normal just so I could go back to being part of that abnormally small percentage of society who has elite athletic skills. However, the bullet in my body introduced doubt into my psyche, and if you're a baseball player who is trying to do the near impossible, which is to hit a baseball going one hundred miles per hour, just a nanosecond of physical or mental doubt could be the difference between success and failure. And that's in the best of circumstances. Yet, I was proud of myself because I'd eventually overcome that doubt to get signed with another Minor League Baseball team, but that's a story for later.

Throughout this period, I was still on television every single day, as the news kept going with the story. The whole "if it bleeds it leads" ethos meant that there was constant interest in the Robbie Tolan story in the Houston area, which meant that my face was easily recognizable. I would constantly meet strangers at the supermarket, in restaurants, or anywhere, and of course I'd be the "Aren't you the guy who was shot?" guy. It was weird; strangers wanted to take pictures with me, as though being shot by the police was enough to turn me into a Houston version of Jay-Z, only with a bullet in his back.

Although I didn't have protest marches in my name, I have to say that my most stalwart allies came from the hospitals. Nurses, doctors, and other people from the hospital used to come by my house to lend their support. And when I talk about support, it was sometimes nothing more than being blessed by people who cared enough to tell me that getting shot wasn't my fault and that having to deal with the aftermath really sucked. I knew they couldn't go out in public and cheerlead for me, but I knew that they were on my team. I mean, on my last day at the hospital, everyone in the hospital who had attended to me, from nurses to staff, came to see me off. You can't overestimate how much those gestures picked up my spirits and made me feel connected with people who empathized with me. Hell, as they lined the walls as I was rolled out in a wheelchair, I felt like Kanye as they cheered!

That was the physical disconnection and the support that came from it. But the psychological detachment wasn't as positive, nor did I know how to plot a course through it. Slowly but surely, the visits stopped and a sense of isolation crept in. I found that people really did have the same attitude as Michael Harris, a sort of "Hey man, you're alive, so that means you're good, right?" As long as people came to see me, I was good because I was distracted from the negative thoughts. But once they stopped, I was left alone with my own demons.

And let me say clearly that that shit was terrible.

From the first night I spent at my Aunt Carolyn's house, I began having nightmares, horrible nightmares where I'd wake up drenched in sweat from head to toe, soaking my sheets on a nightly basis. It got so bad that I began sleeping on one side of the bed, with a set of dry clothes in a chair, all because I knew that every two hours I'd be drenched in sweat.

The more I slept, when I could sleep, the worse the nightmares got. They became more gruesome and more vivid with each hallucination; the details weren't always the same, but they always ended with me being found dead. There was always a vision of me, in an out-of-body experience, looking down at a lifeless me in a casket, while standing right next to my parents who are looking down at me with an inconsolable grief. My subconscious brain would see that, and my body would react by getting physical and violent.

I'd fight my way awake, thrashing, punching, and strangling at the air to the point where it scared everyone in my family as they ran into my bedroom. I became so terrified of closing my eyes, even for a few minutes, that I became a part-time insomniac. I'd convinced myself that if I went to sleep I wouldn't wake up. So only after I became exhausted would I get a few hours of peaceful sleep each night. But by that time, I'd begun to hate myself. How could a young man who'd not had a fear in the world, even when a one-hundred-mile-per-hour baseball was headed at my head, suddenly be frightened about sleeping? What was going on in my life?

I felt like no one around me could help, and I didn't want to throw yet another burden on them, so I began self-diagnosing my problem. I'd been prescribed both Xanax for my anxiety and Vicodin for my pain, and I thought that if I went off both maybe, just maybe, I might be able to stop having the night sweats and nightmares combo platter each night.

Boy, was I wrong.

What happened was that instead of only being able to sleep for a few hours a night, I'd become a *full-time* insomniac. The pain from not taking the Vicodin was so intense that it was nothing for me to stay up for thirty-six to forty-eight hours, just so I could get about three hours of normal sleep. It was a deep sleep that was so all-consuming that my brain apparently couldn't go into nightmare mode. But to me, that was a burden that I was just going to have to deal with.

I saw the trouble that my family was going through, both emotionally and financially, and I felt guilty. It's weird to say that because I hadn't done anything except be the victim, but I thought about it all the time. My brain kept going over alternative scenarios where my family wouldn't have to be burdened with me.

What if I'd just made the decision to stay in that night and not gone out with Anthony? None of this would have happened then, right? But then, my brain would snap back and tell me that nothing should have happened when we did go out, so what would have been the guarantee that the Bellaire police wouldn't have done the same thing a day later or a year later? There was none.

Or what if I'd let Cotton throw my mom against the garage versus standing up for her? Yeah, but I wasn't raised like that, my brain would respond. When you see your tiny little petite mom thrown against the garage, then you react. It's a human response. No, that wasn't my fault, but it was the fault of the cop who shouldn't have escalated the situation.

But my last thought was the darkest one. What if I had been killed by that bullet instead of just injured?

Maybe if I hadn't survived, my family could have just had the funeral, grieved over my death, and then eventually, no matter how painful my loss would have been, moved on with their lives. Instead, now I was living with my Aunt Carolyn and Uncle Charles, who despite the fact that they had already raised all of their own kids, had a new inconvenience in their lives—me.

It got to the point that, because I couldn't sleep and because I felt so guilty, I'd only come out of my bedroom when I was certain that my aunt and uncle were asleep. Despite their kindness and hospitality, I didn't want to be a reminder to them about the burden I was causing.

I also saw the huge amounts of money that everyone was

spending, and it just hurt my soul. I mean we had a bill of over two hundred grand just from the hospital alone, with the private rooms, the tests, and the pills. And then we had almost three hundred thousand dollars in legal fees, and I just thought, "Man, I am the problem at the center of all of this turmoil." And I'm not ashamed to say that I thought about suicide quite often during that period, thinking that it would be so much better for everyone involved if my problems were gone from everyone else's lives. The physical damage and the mental damage were overwhelming.

I ended up going to a psychologist who specializes in trauma, but I never wanted to see a therapist, mainly because I didn't want to hear someone who didn't look like me playing devil's advocate for the police.

"Do you think that if you'd done what the police had asked, you wouldn't have gotten shot?" "If, if, if…" I didn't want to hear any of that. I regret the fact that this shooting caused so much pain and financial issues for my family, and yeah, those questions may bounce around in my own head, but I don't regret a single thing I did that night. I would do it again in a heartbeat.

I tried to create outlets for getting the shit out of my head whenever I got too low. I had people I could talk to, friends and family, but my saving grace was that fact that I also wrote quite a bit in a diary. Writing was therapy for me, and because of that, I didn't want to go to a therapist just to please everyone else. I felt like I had this situation, even with the dark thoughts, handled. Like most of the people in my family, I was independent and proud of it. What would I gain from telling my story to a stranger?

But everyone, especially my mom, kept saying, "You need to

talk to somebody. You need to talk to somebody." I finally gave in and said I would do it. So off to the psychologist I went. The session lasted for about an hour and a half, during which she asked me all types of questions.

"How do you feel?"

"Do you think being shot changed your life?"

"Tell me about the nightmares."

"What do you think about life and living now?"

"What do you think your new normal is now?"

After the session, she told me that it was obvious that I'd gone through something very traumatic (ya think?), and I was either very strong or very good at bullshitting. I told her that it was a little bit of both, and I never went back to her again.

It's not that I'm against therapy, but I just didn't see any value in having a stranger tell me things that I either already knew or had figured out for myself. Plus, there are things that I think you can't analyze simply because you went to school and read about them. Trauma is a very personal experience, and only people who've experienced it can relate, as I'd find out later. But my mom thought otherwise.

My mom thought I was a great bullshitter because when things got dark, when emotions would try to come in, I'd try to crack a joke in order to change the atmosphere. She thought I was just repressing my emotions.

What I decided to do was to concentrate on expressing myself with my writing. I wrote in a journal every day, detailing my thoughts, my emotions, and where I was in the world on any particular day. That proved to be more cathartic than lying on a couch talking to a stranger. I found that I was working it out myself and that I had the answers within me. I believe that because I'd been venting through my diary posts, the dark cloud of depression suddenly lifted, never to return. Like just out of the blue, I wasn't blue anymore, and depression has never touched me again.

However, I'll admit that with hindsight being 20/20 and a slight bit of gallows humor, if I may, maybe I wouldn't have had so many suicidal thoughts if I'd scheduled a few more therapy sessions with her. Writing wasn't the only solution, and maybe I'd have been better off if I'd used a combo plate to deal with my mental issues. But I didn't and I'm still here. Let me repeat: I'm still here.

And that's the ultimate victory.

## CHAPTER 4

# A LONG SERIES OF ISOLATED INCIDENTS

## Victor Steen, 17, Pensacola, Florida—October 3, 2009

Victor Steen, a seventeen-year-old African American teen, was riding his bike when Pensacola officer Jerald Ard chased him down, tasered him from his patrol car window, and then ran over him, killing him instantly. Steen had been nearly torn in half due to the impact from the police car. Officer Ard was then suspected of planting a gun in the pocket of Steen after being seen on video planting an object next to the dead boy. Officer Ard was placed on administrative leave immediately after the death of Steen but returned to plainclothes duty ten days later. Later, the City of Pensacola paid the family $500,000 to settle the case.

learned quickly that in a police shooting drama involving a white officer shooting a black victim, the institutions and organizations associated with the police are going to do their best to protect the white officer. The City of Bellaire and the Bellaire police union wanted to shine the best light possible on Sgt. Cotton. Society looks upon police as doing a tough job, and as such, they are given as much latitude to keep the bad guys away as they need. You know how on Mother's Day, every mother on earth is considered to be the best mother on earth, no matter what? It's just the default premise everyone goes with because no one wants to sully the name of mothers by pointing out that there are some bad mothers who don't love their kids, who cook bad meals, and who sometimes jump in cars with strange men and leave their kids behind for a new life. Well, that's what happens when we talk about the police. No one ever wants to say that police can be bad.

And not only that, but police departments across the country can be corrupt when it comes to violence against black people.

Look, I support the police, but what was said as a way to justify my shooting was downright cruel. Every police officer, even the ones who shoot innocent people, is considered a hero. They put their lives on the line each day to be the thin blue line between criminals and good people. They are the people who run to the disaster and not the people who run away from it. At least that's how they're portrayed, instead of being portrayed as people who may do a tough job, but also do it with the same bigotries, biases, and prejudices that non-policemen have in society. Except police officers carry a deadly weapon, and we depend on them to make good judgments so that the innocent don't get hurt or die as a result. However, in the case of black people, even when the innocent don't do anything at all, their blackness can be enough to get them killed by police.

Take for example the tragic death of Philando Castile, a regular black guy who lived in St. Paul, Minnesota. By all the news accounts that I saw, Philando loved being in his community. He worked as a nutrition services supervisor at J. J. Hill Montessori Magnet School, and when the school staff and students were interviewed, it was clear that he was beloved. I mean, the guy had a tattoo of the Twin Cities. What else do you need?

So Castile is driving, with his girlfriend Field Reynolds in the passenger seat and her four-year-old daughter in the backseat, when his car gets stopped for a broken taillight by St. Anthony, Minnesota, police officers Jeronimo Yanez and Joseph Kauser. Fine. It should be a routine stop. Write the fix-it ticket, and then everyone goes on their way. But it didn't go that way, just like Jose Cruz's stop didn't go that way. We know that because we saw the aftermath when Field Reynolds logged into Facebook Live to show Yanez's gun still pointed at a dying Castile; her calm voice says, "We got pulled over for a busted taillight in the back and the police...just killed my boyfriend."

According to the police dash cam, Officer Yanez walks to the driver side where he asks Castile for his ID. Castile, in a very clear and calm voice, lets the officer know that he's carrying a firearm, for which he has a legal permit.

"Sir, I have to tell you, I do have a firearm on me," Castile said.

"Okay," said Yanez. "Okay, don't reach for it."

"I'm reaching for...," Castile started, as he reached for his ID.

"Don't pull it out!" Yanez said, suddenly taking out his weapon and pointing it at Castile. His partner, Officer Kauser, stands to the side, calm. He shows no concern or sense that they're in danger. Castile, still trying to be calm, tries to explain.

"I'm not pulling it out," Castile says, still calm and still measured.

"Don't pull it out!" yells Yanez, who is clearly out of control. Suddenly, Yanez fires seven times at point-blank range at Castile, hitting him five times, twice through the heart. One bullet hits the console and barely misses Reynolds, and the other misses the four-year-old daughter in the backseat by inches.

What's amazing about this situation is that Reynolds knew that in order to preserve her own life, she had to tamp down her emotions as much as possible, so she calmly described the horrific scene to a live Facebook audience, all while interacting with a hyperventilating Yanez.

"I told him not to reach for it! I told him to get his head up!" Yanez yelled, still out of control, his breathing rapid and deep.

"He had," Reynolds said calmly, "told him to get his ID, sir, his driver's license. Oh my God, please don't you tell me he's dead."

"Fuck."

"Please don't tell me my boyfriend just went like that."

"Keep your hands where they are please," Yanez commanded.

"Yes I will, sir," Reynolds said, as she tried to keep calm and also calm her four-year-old daughter who'd just seen her mother's boyfriend murdered.

"I will keep my hands where they are. Please don't tell me this. Lord, please Jesus, don't tell me that he's gone. Please don't tell me that he's gone. Please officer, don't tell me that you just did this to him. You shot four bullets into him, sir. He was just getting his license and registration, sir."

After the police took Reynolds out of the car and placed her and her four-year-old daughter into the back of the police car, the scared four-year-old pleaded for calm.

"Mom, please stop saying cuss words and screaming because I don't want you to get shooted," the girl said. Reynolds gave her a kiss.

"I could keep you safe," her daughter said.

It's heartbreaking. An innocent black man was killed for doing nothing but having a broken taillight. And it was all on camera. And yet, when Yanez went to trial for second-degree manslaughter, he pulled out the same old canard that police officers everywhere use when shooting black people.

I was scared for my life.

"I know he had an object and it was dark," Yanez said during his deposition. "And he was pulling it out with his right hand. And as he was pulling it out I, a million things started going through my head. And I thought I was gonna die. And, I was scared because, I didn't know if he was gonna, I didn't know what he was gonna do. He just had somethin' uh his hands and he, the first words that he said to me were, some of the first words he said is that he had a gun. And I thought he was reaching for the gun. I thought he had the gun in his hand, in his right hand. And I thought he had it enough to where all he had to do is just pull it out, point it at me, move his trigger finger down on the trigger and let off rounds. And I had no other option than, to take out my firearm and, and I shot. Um I shot him."

And guess what? Despite the fact that it was on video and that anyone could see that Castile posed no threat and that Yanez had panicked for no reason, a jury found Yanez not guilty. The jury bought the idea that Yanez was reasonably scared and that was enough reason to murder Castile. Castile as the dead black man in this case was considered to be guilty by his very existence, and therefore, a huge hurdle would need to be cleared for Yanez to be convicted. And not even the apparent innocence of Castile could do it.

To a certain extent, that's what happened with me. As a black man, I was considered guilty until proven innocent, just like Castile, and it was as though the public needed to find something they could pin on me as a justification for Sgt. Cotton pulling the trigger. Let's say that it had come out that in the past that I had not paid a traffic ticket; in the eyes of some people, that would have been enough rationalization for me getting a bullet to the chest. For Castile, some people justified his death by pointing out that he'd been stopped fifty-two times for minor traffic infractions, as though being a bad driver was a reasonable excuse for being blasted by a cop.

Hell, despite the fact that I'd received a lot of support, I still had people play on racial stereotypes, saying that my family and I were on welfare, from the ghetto, and uneducated, to justify why I shouldn't speak out about my shooting. Others said that we were just out here to get rich from a payday, as though it made logical sense to get shot in order to make a lot of money. Who would do that? I was used to fans booing me because I'd struck out or made an error in the field, but I couldn't fathom why people who didn't know me would concoct these racist fantasies as a way to justify Sgt. Cotton shooting me. Maybe it's because I was raised to treat everyone with respect and kindness that breaking out of that utopian bubble meant that I was shocked to realize that the real world is often cruel and nonsympathetic.

Because of this kind of thinking, I believe we as African Americans get tied up in an unwinnable game of trying to make sure that the black victims of gun violence at the hands of the police are portrayed as being beyond reproach. We want to let the world know that the person who was killed had so many positive attributes that they didn't *deserve* to die—not just during the incident, like pointing out that Philando Castile had followed every single direction, but afterward.

A white supremacist society looks at blackness as criminal, and so it will do everything from turning a seventeen-year-old Trayvon Martin into a menacing black teen monster to calling the black victim a thug. At the same time, the society will infantilize a white man who is well beyond eighteen years old as a "kid." I remember watching the 2016 Summer Olympics in Brazil and hearing people call the US Olympic swimmer Ryan Lochte a "kid" as they tried to justify him allegedly vandalizing a gas station and lying about having been robbed. He was thirty-two years old. So as compensation, we as black people go to great lengths to prove the virtue of black victims of police violence, which plays right into the white supremacist trap.

Every positive characteristic that could be used to show me as undeserving of being shot was used. I was a Christian and a talented baseball player. I loved my mother. And all of those things were true. But even if I'd been a person with a prison record, who didn't like my mother, and basically was an unlikeable person, I would have had the exact same right to not be shot. By playing into this notion that my goodness was the key to my righteousness tacitly told the world that there *were* some black people who did deserve to be shot by the police. The poor. The inarticulate. The ones with funny names like Alize and Shenequa. The vulnerable. The ones with low-hanging pants. If I had to demonstrate that I was a stellar person in order to prove that my being shot was a tragedy, then I was saying that the non-stellar black people were on their own. I reject that, and it's a fallacy.

When I did one of my first media appearances, I remember one reporter asking, "What advice would you give a young kid, who is a good kid and follows the rules like yourself, but who feels that because something like this happens to a person like you, he's now lost faith in our law enforcement and justice system? What would you say to him?"

This question still troubles me. I paused while I tried to calculate an answer. It seemed to be the longest couple of seconds of silence. Finally, I simply said, "Ma'am, I really don't know, I'm sorry."

Her face seemed to show disappointment with my answer, but

then again, what was the answer? Was I supposed to tell this kid to have blind faith in a system that regularly shot and killed black people like myself? Where does this wondrous faith come from? I knew my answer was unsatisfactory, but it was only unsatisfactory because there was no good answer. Telling a young kid to stay on a righteous path is good advice, but it's not the answer for staying safe. Black people like myself had been killed by the police for walking home, for driving, for walking across the street, for making an illegal lane change, for having their car break down in the middle of the highway, and for simply existing in a space that the white police officer thought they shouldn't. So how do you come up with an answer for that type of scenario?

I remember when a young black country music singer wanted to make a name for himself, and to get some clicks, he created an "instructional" video for black people on how to not get shot by the police. It was so absurd, and yet when I read the comments, it reinforced my belief that white people think that black people get shot because we're too dumb to follow directions, so as a result, we deserve it. That's the system we have.

More importantly, why do Americans want to be reassured that, despite the injustice foisted upon me, I still have faith in a law enforcement system and criminal justice system that failed me? Is it because it protects them, and therefore, although they feel bad that I had suffered because of it, they think the overall goodness of the system works for everyone? Do they think the black bodies lying in the streets are simply an unfortunate series of isolated incidents and that black people should still believe police officers have our best interests at heart? I don't believe that.

The question bothered me for a long time after it had been

asked, to the point where decided to write an online blog post about it.

*My entire life I had to keep my nose clean. I was a good student and a pretty good athlete. Never touched a drop of alcohol, minus the annual glass of New Year's Eve champagne with the family, until I turned 21. I've never smoked, done drugs, and I've never been arrested. I've never been in any kind of major trouble...*

*I care about people and I love my family to death. I like to make people laugh. When I can help someone out, or put a smile on his or her face, it makes my heart smile. And ever since I can remember, I've wanted nothing more than to play baseball; that is my heart.*

*Being the son of a former Major League veteran, I'm used to the doubt and criticism. It's been there my entire life. I can handle that. But I was shot in the chest for simply protecting my rights and my parents' rights, which is much different. I can live with and accept a lot of things; however, injustice will never be one of them. All my life, I've never done anything to anyone, but strangers who didn't even know me have had mean and hateful things to say about me. I've received death threats, with many of them believing I "deserved what I got." And some of them, the truly awful ones, even felt like I deserved more than what I got.*

*Understand that I will never throw myself, nor ask for, a pity party. But do realize that there are just some people who just want to be hateful for the sake of being hateful. Many people just want everyone else to be as miserable as them. And that's fine, I may not like it, but I can accept it.*

*What I do realize is that despite keeping my nose clean my entire life, people talked about me. Despite never being in any kind of trouble, people talked about me. Despite being a good kid, people talked about me. So, after being shot in the chest for refusing to lay down while a cop manhandled my mother; after I flat lined on December 31, 2008, at approximately 2:31 a.m.; after being accused of stealing my own car and driving it to my own house; after all the evidence pointed out my innocence and the officer's guilt...people STILL talked about me.*

*I'm damned if I do, and damned if I don't. So please pay close attention to what I'm about to say because this is me and my most honest; no ego, no arrogance, just one hundred percent genuine...*

*I don't care about what anyone thinks of me anymore.*

And to this day, I still don't care what people think of me, with no apologies.

But my character didn't matter when it came to the white officer Sgt. Cotton. Regardless of whether the statements were true or false, the goal was to create a narrative maintaining that Sgt. Cotton was a standup guy who hadn't made a mistake in shooting me, but had made a judgment call that any "reasonable" officer would have made. Bellaire officials tried to paint him as a choirboy, someone who'd never been in trouble, and claimed that my shooting was just an unfortunate aberration. But my lawyers had done their research. Plus, as it turned out, so had the Harris County District Attorney's Office.

The Harris County District Attorney's Office turned out to be a real ally in our fight for justice in the criminal case, and it was led by two prosecutors for the case, Clint Greenwood and Steven Morris. Soon after the indictment, they asked to meet with me and my family. Their message? Keep telling the truth, no matter what. Nothing compromises a case more than finding inconsistencies in a victim's story, especially when most juries and judges tend to trust the judgment of police officers who have shot people. We couldn't afford any slip-ups. To even have a remote chance at getting justice when you are a black person accusing a police officer, you had to be as perfect as possible. To be a white officer, well, you just did what you thought you needed to do, even if you lied.

"We've gone over countless videos, pictures, and testimonies, and none of your stories have changed," they told us. "Those guys from Bellaire have flip-flopped stories all over the place. Plus, you all are good people. You're not the raging maniacs that the City of Bellaire is trying to make people believe you are."

It was then that we began to have faith that the District Attorney's Office was truly behind the Tolan family. They gave us hope that the criminal justice system, even with all of its racial bias against black shooting victims, just might work for the justice we were seeking. Plus, we had right on our side. No matter how many times we'd been interviewed, we told the same story. Cotton and Edwards? They kept changing their story to make it appear like they weren't the aggressors but the true victims in this saga. Something else also raised our opinions of the prosecutors. They wanted to do an experiment to prove that Cotton was lying.

As it turned out, Cotton had been proclaiming in his depositions that he'd warned me over and over to lie back on the ground, which we disputed. I wasn't given any such order, and Cotton claimed that it took five seconds from the time I got to my knees after seeing my mom thrown against the garage until I was shot. He said that I'd gotten up from the ground and run at him, as he commanded that I get back on the ground. He also claimed he took several steps back.

This was a lie. I'd only gotten to one knee before Cotton shot me. Yet, in an incident like the one that night where an officer is supposed to be making life-and-death decisions without much time to think, five seconds is an eternity. The prosecutors wanted to disprove Cotton's testimony by showing that Cotton had shot me in around two seconds, thus never giving me multiple commands to get on the ground. To do that, we needed to do a re-enactment that was credible to a jury.

"Robbie, you wouldn't still have the same shoes you wore that night?" Greenwood asked.

"I do," I said, as I got up from the dining room table to retrieve them. In the back of my closet was a plastic bag with faded teal letters that read "Ben Taub Hospital," and inside that bag contained everything the nurses had stripped off me on the night of the shooting: socks, the bloodied pants that were cut off me in the operating room, my earring and necklace, and the gray, black, and orange Nike Air Force One shoes I had on when I was shot. The bag hadn't been opened in nearly a year. My parents had showed it to me right after the *Real Sports with Bryant Gumbel* interview, but I couldn't stand to see the bloodied pants, so I never opened it. But for Greenwood and Morris, it was golden that I'd kept them.

"We want to be as thorough and accurate as possible," they told us. A few days later, Keith Webb, who'd done most of the preliminary depositions, joined them with dozens of photos. The idea was that, in order to re-create what happened, they needed to make sure they knew exactly where my body was in contrast to Cotton, and that meant checking at least ten different pictures of the same blood-soaked doormat. My testimony had to match what Webb saw as an expert in ballistics. Together, our testimony could show Cotton's exact position based on the angle of where the three shots were fired and where one of the shots entered my chest.

During the re-creations, Greenwood played the role of Cotton, while Morris played the role of my mom. The idea was for me to jump up and immediately run at Greenwood, just as Cotton claimed in his deposition, as Greenwood somehow instinctively shoved Morris, playing my mom, into the garage, while at the same time pulling out his gun, commanding me to get back on the ground, and taking steps back.

"He's pretty fast," Cotton said in his deposition when asked about the five seconds it took for me to jump up and run at him. We wanted to do a re-creation to demonstrate that Cotton was lying through his teeth. Also, Cotton wanted to make it appear that he was fearful of being overrun, while at the same time making sure to give me enough warning to stop. But he seemed confused during his deposition about why he felt fearful of me trying to stand up.

"It's everything together, I couldn't give a—like a list that would say all of these different things, because there's all sorts of factors that you're kind of analyzing and—and seeing stuff as you go along," Cotton said. "So I really—I couldn't—I couldn't say that this list is an all-inclusive list of—of what made me feel that way. Well, not in and of itself, I mean, there—everything together made me believe that, yes. That was one of the things."

Webb set up the scene outside the house and then marked everyone's place on the concrete. Greenwood took the clip out of his gun before the reenactment, showing everyone that it was empty, and yeah, that wasn't an attempt at a funny joke; he wanted to make sure that nothing dumb happened again.

The reenactment reminded me of baseball practice. We did a slow walkthrough of the drill twice before we did at full speed. Five seconds was the magic number because Cotton was so adamant about everything taking five seconds. Again, he wanted to prove that he gave me several commands to get back down during that time, but that, instead, I jumped up and ran at him, giving him no option but to shoot. Webb stood off to the side with the stopwatch ready to record the time.

"Robbie," Clint asked, "I know you're about to play baseball this year, but how good of shape were you in then? Had you been working out?"

"Probably better shape," I responded wryly. "I hadn't been shot."

"Okay, let's do this," Greenwood said.

Over and over, we re-created that night, and each time gave me shudders. I knew that I had to climb this mental mountain to reach the summit of justice, but damn, if it wasn't hard. But I did it. Over and over until Morris told us we were done.

"There's no way Cotton was telling the truth," Morris concluded. "He kept saying that he gave you several commands to get back down, and that just doesn't pass the smell test."

"No way," Greenwood said. "No way it took you five seconds to jump up and run at him. I mean, everything is happening too fast. If I'm pushing your mother, taking my gun out, aiming it, telling you to stop, and *then* taking steps back at the same time? No."

Webb had been keeping track of the times, and they were

consistent with my testimony. Each time we'd run through the drill, I was in Greenwood's face in less than two seconds. Before he could say, "Stop," he and I were nose to nose. My slowest time was 1.6 seconds, not 5 seconds. This meant that what I said was true. I'd gotten to one knee, and then he shot me.

"And I did all of my movements because I *knew* to do it. It was premeditated," Greenwood said. "There's no way Cotton did all of that instinctively in that amount of time. There's no way he's telling the truth."

"Why don't we videotape the re-creation for the trial?" I asked.

"If we did that," Greenwood explained, "then we'd have to enter it into evidence. I'm thinking that I want to do the demonstration live in the courtroom so they won't know what hit 'em." And so with that, Greenwood and Morris were ready to present our case. As for me, I needed to get back to working toward my pre-shooting self.

Part of my rehabilitation for getting back to normal meant getting back to doing what I loved to do, which was to play baseball. When I was in the hospital, and then doing rehab at Aunt Carolyn's house, baseball seemed like a distant memory, almost like an impossible dream. The idea of hitting a baseball when I was simply trying to breathe on one lung was ridiculous. Running around the bases with speed and precision? A ludicrous idea when I needed a walker and someone behind me, just to protect me from falling over. Hell, I couldn't even go to the bathroom by myself. I was as far away from playing baseball as Jeffrey Cotton was from being named Man of the Year by Black Lives Matter.

But then, through hard work and a lot of pain, I began getting better. After a year of small steps, the dream of baseball began replacing the nightmare of getting shot. I needed a path back, someone to believe in me, and to be honest, I didn't know where to find that person. But I have this belief that if you're a good person who does things for others, eventually the universe and God will look out for you. And soon Dmitri Young came back into my life.

You know how kids go to their parents' office on "Bring Your Kid to Work Day"? Well, it just so happened that my dad's office was the Major League dugouts and clubhouses, so I was always meeting players when they came to play the Houston Astros. Even though Dmitri Young played for the Cincinnati Reds, we became quick friends, to the point where I'd nicknamed him DY. That's a big deal when you're a twelve- or thirteen-year-old snot-nosed kid who dreams of being like your baseball heroes. I didn't just know Dmitri Young; he was DY!

Dmitri was amazingly down to earth, even to a little kid. In a sport where you can be "on" all the time, you know, have a public persona that is hard to penetrate because you don't want people to know the real you, Dmitri wasn't that guy. His personality was approachable, and he always had time for me. I was sad when he was traded to the Detroit Tigers because it meant that we wouldn't be able to see each other as often. This was before interleague play, and since the Tigers are in the American League and the Houston Astros were, at the time, in the National League, it was like I was on Earth and Dmitri was on Mars. But then, one day, we saw each other at an annual conference, and that was my path back to baseball.

The Baseball Assistance Team, or B.A.T., is a nonprofit organization designed to help current and former baseball players tackle financial and medical hardships. Not all Major League Baseball players, like my dad for instance, were able to take advantage of the multi-million-dollar contracts that came through free agency in the 1980s to today. My dad made enough to be comfortable, but like many players from the 1960s and 1970s, he still worked during the off season. In fact, my dad still works to this day, sometimes as an Uber driver, just to make ends meet.

So every year, usually around January, B.A.T. holds a large fundraiser in New York City called Going to Bat for B.A.T. We typically go each year, but obviously, because I was shot on New Year's Eve of 2008, I missed the 2009 meeting while I recovered in the hospital. But I was eager to go to the next fundraiser, because it is a cavalcade of Major League stars, including dozens of Hall of Famers, and since I'd grown up with them, I knew they'd be interested in seeing that I was okay. Plus, it's truly an amazing and inspiring experience. You never get tired of being surrounded by your heroes.

The event consists of a cocktail party for players and guests only, followed by a silent auction and autograph session with the fans, and then dinner. It's a time for fellowship, reminiscing about their playing days, and generally catching up with each other. I'd known most of these men for all of my life, so they were like family. Yes, they were a very famous family but part of my extended family nonetheless.

By the time I sat down for the B.A.T. dinner in 2010, I knew I was ready to return to baseball, but again, the path wasn't clear on how I'd get there. The independent Bay Area Toros had released me back in 2008, so even when I was healthy, I was fighting an uphill battle to stay in the game. But a combination of my frustration over the continued postponement of the trial and a fierce determination to get back in baseball shape meant that after a full year of rehab, I felt like I was back in baseball shape.

I was motivated, running and working out with a minimum of pain, and that meant I had control over my body again. Something happens mentally when you're back in control of your body, your functions, and what you can do, and I think that it helped make the world an optimistic place for me, even with the trial still awaiting. And I believe that others can sense optimism, which is why I think Dmitri approached me at the 2010 B.A.T. dinner.

"Hey man, can you do me a favor and take these baseball cards," he asked, handing me a large stack of baseball cards, "and get some of these guys to sign them?" The autograph table was packed full of famous players signing cards for fans, which meant that the players themselves couldn't get autographs for their own cards. And since Dmitri was a huge baseball card collector, I didn't mind doing it. I had access the fans didn't have, meaning that I could go behind ropes and security and get access to anyone I wanted.

After the dinner, I met up with Dmitri to give him back his signed cards, and while he was thanking me, he asked, "Didn't see you here last year, man. Where you been?" It was funny, but Dmitri was the first person in the past 365 days who didn't know that I'd been shot, and it was damn refreshing. To him, I was just the now grown up dude who used to be his twelve-year-old friend, nothing more or less. When I told him what happened, he was enraged and nearly in tears. We talked for hours about what I'd been doing to get back to normal and how my road had been rocky. Dmitri had recently retired, which I've heard is like death to athletes, and so I think he was even more attuned to what it meant to not be able to do what you want to on the athletic field due to injury beyond your control.

I left the conference feeling good about having seen him, but I wasn't expecting any further contact. But then, a few weeks after the dinner, Dmitri sent me a series of text messages.

"Hey, can you run?"

"Yeah."

"Are you all healed up? Can you work out, hit, and throw?"

"Hell yeah," I replied, slowly coming to the realization that Dmitri was trying to see if he had a ball player on his phone or someone who just used to be a ball player. There's a difference. Slowly, I began getting excited. I didn't know what DY was going to be able to do, but I did know that faith and hope mean that anything is possible. He called me later.

"So I'm now working for a team in the Frontier League, an independent squad called the Oakland County Cruisers," Dmitri said during our conversation. "I'm now the vice president of base-ball operations, and my first order of business is to get you back on the field."

In less than an hour, my path back to baseball had been laid, and my jaw dropped when Dmitri explained the opportunity to me. It was everything I could have asked for, which was nothing but a chance. When you don't have that chance, you feel so empty, and that was part of the collateral damage that Cotton's bullet had caused. It seemed to take away my chances. The ship that had sailed was only where the bullet had entered my body, but it sure as hell tried to infect my brain with doubt about whether I'd ever get another chance to do what I loved.

Because Dmitri had been impressed by my tenacity in rehabbing and overcoming my injuries, he wanted to take a chance on me. That meant that regardless of whether I stuck on the team or flamed out as a baseball player, from that moment on, I'd won. I'd beaten that damn bullet. Now I needed to see if I could win this criminal trial against Cotton.

# CHAPTER 5

# THE TRIAL OF MY LIFE

## Aiyana Stanley-Jones, 7, Detroit, Michigan—May 16, 2010

Aiyana Stanley-Jones, a seven-year-old African American girl, was asleep on the couch when Detroit's Special Response Unit, the city's SWAT team, burst into her home around midnight. With the reality crime show *The First 48* in tow, Officer Joseph Weekley threw a flash bang grenade into the house, and then fired a single shot from his weapon, hitting Jones in the back of the head, killing her instantly. Compounding the mistake, they had entered the wrong apartment. Officer Joseph Weekley was charged with involuntary manslaughter and reckless endangerment with a gun. After two trials, Officer Weekley was cleared on all counts.

All I remember was leaving our courtroom, the courtroom where Cotton's defense attorneys had patted him on the back with congratulations, walking into another room, and collapsing into a ball. There I was in the fetal position, weeping uncontrollably. My parents really couldn't do or say anything, and the rest of my family just let me be. When the verdict of not guilty was read, my brain went blank, in the same way it had gone blank when I'd been shot. I've heard victims talk about being traumatized by the criminal justice system, and now I understand. A jury of my peers had looked at the evidence and had basically said to me, "You deserved that bullet."

And I couldn't handle it. But let me back up a bit.

After a year of waiting, postponements, and just plain delaying tactics, the trial finally started during the first week of May 2010, over a year and a half after I was shot. I was feeling fairly confident about the case Greenwood and Morris were going to present. The reenactments were solid. The evidence was there. I wasn't an expert on how to prosecute a case against police officers, but we'd done everything we'd been asked. We'd been truthful, but more importantly, we believed that, like everything else, this was in God's hands, and He wouldn't let us down. After all, we'd gotten miracles already: I was alive, and we'd gotten an indictment. Why would a conviction be a bridge too far?

My relatives and supporters would come out in droves to the courtroom on the first day of the trial, which was reserved for something called voir dire. I had no idea what voir dire meant, but Greenwood and Morris explained that it was Latin from the phrase, *verum dicere*, which means, "that which is true." Initially, it referred to the oath that the jury took to be impartial, but now it refers to the process of picking and swearing in the jury. This process took all day, but Greenwood and Morris made sure to make themselves available to us day and night for any questions we had.

I was worried about the jury more than anything else. Remember those death threats? I said that I wasn't worried about that specific person trying to kill me, but I was worried that one of those types of people could be on the jury. And it only took one—just one person who looked at my black skin and saw nothing but the racism they'd learned and grew up with all of their lives and who had none of the empathy I needed for someone to see the evidence clearly.

Around six o'clock in the evening, the jury had been picked, and Greenwood explained that neither side would get the exact people they wanted. It would be a mix of people who believed that the police should have wide latitude in cases like mine and others who think people of color get a raw deal. The job of Greenwood and Morris would be to prove that Cotton had violated my civil rights, hadn't been truthful in his deposition testimony, and as a result, was guilty of aggravated assault. And even if they had a jury box full of indifferent or middle-of-the-road jurors, I was confident that we'd prove our case.

I guess that's the ultimate answer to the woman who asked about how the little kid could still have hope that the system is just. Regardless of what I'd gone through, call me crazy, but I still believed in the goodness of America to do right by me. Yeah, I knew the statistics, but deep in my gut, I thought that Americans could see my situation for what it was and get justice for me. They say Americans are the ultimate optimists, and I think that perhaps I'm just like everyone else.

The night before the trial began with a jury, I was back to being the insomniac I was after leaving the hospital. The media was swarming again, we were all over the television news each night, and I felt like I was in a fishbowl again. I felt like I was suddenly reliving a nightmare. I can't emphasize how much your anonymity, your privacy, should be guarded and valued. Because when you lose it, you feel like you're stripped naked before the world.

In the early morning hours on the day of the trial, I sat in my bedroom with my back against the wall, staring at the suit I'd chosen to wear. It was freshly cleaned, still in the plastic protective bag. As much as I'd wanted this day to come, with the two postponements making it feel like it would never come, a small part of me wanted another postponement—something that would delay the inevitable for the third time, so I wouldn't have to face it. As much as I wanted to look Jeffrey Cotton in the eye and let him know that, despite his efforts, I not only survived, but was going to thrive and that he needed to pay for what he'd done, I'll have to admit that I was also terrified. I wanted to crawl back into the safety of that hospital bubble and be Unknown 90, that vulnerable young man the nurses and doctors had protected from the outside world. Every transition, from me leaving the hospital to going to my Aunt Carolyn's to starting the trial, had created this yearning need for anonymity.

So as the minutes ticked toward the inevitable, I tried to escape by listening to jazz. Involuntary tears began to roll down from the corners of my eyes. It's awful to be scared shitless and not be able to express it to anyone, all because they need to see you strong, and I was scared shitless. That's what it's like to be trapped.

Around six in the morning, I heard the alarm go off in my aunt and uncle's bedroom. Wide awake, I let out a resigned sigh and lifted my head from the wall. Minutes later, Aunt Carolyn walked down the hall and poked her head into my bedroom.

"Time to get up, Robbie. You've got to get ready."

"I'm up," I said, my monotone voice betraying my lack of enthusiasm for the task ahead. I willed myself to the shower, and let the water flow over me longer than normal, as though I was trying to cleanse myself. I watched the water run down my body, a body now scarred from my sternum to my belly button, and I got angry. I felt around to my back, where the bullet had traveled after leaving my liver. It was then that I started praying. The water was now a baptismal soaking, a rejuvenation and new life all in one. As I got out of the shower and got dressed, I suddenly felt more resolve and determination. I wasn't alone in this ordeal, dammit, and I was going to win.

To get through this, I knew that I needed solidarity everywhere I looked. For all of the strength that I projected, I needed as many invisible friendly hands holding me up as possible. I was extremely vulnerable, and I knew it, but I did have my family, and they were going to be my shield and armor. Dozens of them told me that they wanted to come to the trial to support me, and I was good with that, as long as they were there on time. This was not the time to create distractions that either broke my concentration at the task at hand or created additional stress. I didn't need some aunt or uncle or cousin causing a scene, all because they'd gotten stuck in traffic and were now mad that a court officer wasn't letting them in. Get there on time or don't come was my message.

We parked in an underground garage a couple of blocks away from the courthouse, and to my delight, all of my relatives were prompt and accounted for. Several cars, filled to capacity with relatives, were parked side by side in the garage. It picked up my spirits to be surrounded by them as I walked to the courtroom. The rest of the world might judge me by my skin color, but these people loved me.

The courthouse was about two blocks away, and honestly, you'd think that after nearly two years of dealing with this I'd have a handle on the media frenzy that's surrounded my shooting from the start, but I didn't. I still thought that I could walk the streets of Houston anonymously, but the two-block walk to the courthouse proved me wrong. Dozens of Houstonians pointed and stared as I made the slow walk to the trial, with dozens of relatives in tow. I tried to not look anyone directly in the eyes, but I could see people pointing and whispering as we walked. By the time we made it to the courthouse steps, the madness had ratcheted up to eleven, as the reporters, photographers, and television news talking heads descended upon us. It was your typical media circus, and I was the reluctant dude in the middle of it.

I remember walking into the courthouse and thinking that for all of this drama, I'd never seen the inside of a real courthouse in real life. Everything I'd seen of courtrooms had come from episodes of *Law & Order* or *The First 48*, and the reality that my case was just one of many that day struck me as we walked to our courtroom. The ground floor was a crowded lobby full of the accused and the victims waiting on wooden benches, uniformed police drinking coffee, bedraggled lawyers in ill-fitting suits, people waiting to clear their traffic tickets, and, on this day, the media. All of them moved to and fro believing that their concerns were the most important of the day at the courthouse.

Ten minutes after going through security, I was split off from my extended family. Greenwood and Morris wanted my parents, my cousin Anthony, my Aunt Carolyn and Uncle Charles, and me to head to the District Attorney's office, while everyone else scrambled for seats in the packed courtroom.

As we waited in the DA's office, not much was said because there really wasn't much to say. Small talk really isn't appropriate when it comes to a trial, so we sat waiting for Greenwood and Morris. When they arrived, they greeted everyone as if they'd known us for years, which did a lot to relieve the tension in the room.

The judge in my case was Judge Mary Lou Keel, a former

prosecutor in the Harris County District Attorney's Office, so we felt good about having the trial in her courtroom. However, she made a decision that would impact how we'd view the trial, or more accurately, how we couldn't view the trial.

"The judge has invoked the rule in your case," Greenwood explained.

"What's that?" I asked, not sure about any new rules being added at this moment.

"The family is to be secluded from the trial until you all testify," he explained. "It's designed to keep witnesses from being tainted by the testimony of another witness. Since you all were there at the scene, you all have different perspectives on what happened. What we don't want you to do is to suddenly start adding details from something you heard in court."

So in essence, we could all be present together in a room, but we couldn't watch each other give testimony. That seemed reasonable, and since we weren't worried about our various stories, we simply followed our new liaison, Maria, to the top floor of the courtroom to an isolated witness room.

The seclusion room was dark, being poorly lit seemingly on purpose. The room was protected with a guard, and you could only enter after being buzzed in. As we walked into the room, I noticed that they'd assigned an attendant to sit at a desk directly across from the door. Before I sat down, I amused myself by thinking that I was probably in a room that had previously been used to keep mob snitches and corporate whistleblowers safe.

Filled with board games, puzzles, toys, and video games, it seemed like our room also doubled as a day care center for antsy kids. But for adults looking to burn off eight hours worth of anxiety, it wasn't optimal. My cousin Anthony and I hooked up the Nintendo and started playing, while my dad tried to nap. My mom came prepared with a book.

We knew that we were unlikely to testify during the first few days of the trial. Greenwood and Morris had told us that they first had to build the case.

"They got in over their head and panicked," Greenwood began his argument to the jury.

Our liaison, Maria, would periodically leave us and go sit in the courtroom and then come back to bring us vague reports about how things were going. She couldn't tell us about the specific testimony, but she did say that it appeared that Greenwood and Morris were putting on a strong case. She also cheered us by saying that the defense seemed to look weak and unprepared, with the judge seemingly more favorable to the prosecution. Now you have to take all of that with a grain of salt because I'm assuming Maria knew as much about the legal system as we did, but it did keep our spirits up.

The early days of the trial fell into a regular monotony of arriving at the courthouse, eating lunch with my family, and getting bored. My relatives kept attending in droves, but when we got together, they weren't allowed to discuss any details of the case. However, they were taking copious notes that they assured us they'd share after the trial.

News cameras weren't allowed into my courtroom, but they were everywhere in the hallways just outside the courtroom doors. Whenever we needed to use the elevators to get lunch, use the restroom, or anything, you could hear the photographers scramble to get a great shot of the Tolan family. Again, we were living in a fish bowl.

From what I learned after the trial, the second day consisted of the technical aspects and the gruesome details of what happened the night I was shot. According to my relatives, the entire courtroom was filled with dozens of blown up diagrams, pictures of our bloodied doorstep, the bullet holes in our roof, and the gaping hole in my chest, along with the thirty-eight staples holding my stomach together. It's funny, but I remember that day quite clearly because when I saw my relatives, they all had puffy eyes and red noses from crying, but they couldn't tell me what had happened.

"They played the video from one of the dash cams," they told us later. "We could hear you moaning in pain, Marian praying; it was really hard to hear."

Something happens when a shooting moves from being theory, or a story that you read in the newspapers, to real. And although I wasn't interested in going into a courtroom full of people who felt sorry for me, I did want them to be impacted by the devastation that Cotton's actions had caused. My relatives loved me, so that's why they reacted the way they did. Could twelve strangers feel the same?

One critical aspect of the trial centered on the lapel microphones that the Bellaire police officers were wearing that night. In the nearly two years since I'd been shot, the one consistent thing current and ex-cops would say to me when talking about the situation was that the lapel microphones would be crucial to the case.

"The lapel microphone will tell the story of what really

happened," they'd always say. They told me that they were trained to turn on their microphone in any encounter like this, not to protect me, but to protect them against false allegations. At least that's the theory.

It's the same theory people have behind body cameras on cops. The idea is that if police officers know that their actions are being recorded, then they'll make sure to change their behavior. I don't know about that. First, we keep getting video footage from those body cams of black and brown people being shot and killed, so it doesn't seem to be that big of a deterrent. If you're gonna shoot someone because blackness makes you afraid, a body cam ain't gonna make a damn bit of difference.

Second, and this is what I'd love to ask the experts, doesn't the existence of body cams, and lapel microphones for that matter, show that there's a systemic issue with the type of training we're giving this nation's police force and that it would be much better to address the racial biases that cause them to pull out their weapon in the first place? I know that would have helped me.

Regardless, the lapel mics weren't magic elixirs for my case. Neither Cotton nor Edwards had his microphone turned on during our encounter, and after I'd been shot, they turned their mics on and off as they talked with other officers. For example, Cotton turned his microphone on to ask me, "What were you reaching for?" and then turned it off when I answered, "Nothing." You can't tell me that was just an unlucky coincidence that Cotton wanted to get it into the record that he thought that I was reaching for something, while conveniently not recording my answer.

Also, did you catch that? The question about a black man

reaching for something and it turning out to be nothing is the same thing that has happened in other cases, like the Philando Castile case. It's easy to see the pattern if you're not blinded by the notion that police officers have a right to be scared because they have a tough job.

On the third day of the trial, the prosecution finally said that we were going to be called to the witness stand. The four of us had gotten beyond bored sitting in that children's–witness playroom, and we couldn't wait for Maria to come in and let us know it was our turn. Suddenly, the buzzer sounded, and Maria stepped into the room.

"Bobby, they're ready for you."

My dad looked at me and grinned, while putting on his jacket. Honestly, his grin disturbed me more than anything because I knew that he was only doing that because he wanted to make me feel like there wasn't anything to worry about, but I knew better. I still wanted to protect him from this whole thing. This thing that had caused him to have a double bypass due to the stress of watching his son get shot, and who knew what would happen on the stand?

\*　　\*　　\*

I loathed the idea that the defense team was going to get a chance to interrogate my dad. To me, the defense team was an extension of the Bellaire Police Department and the City of Bellaire, two entities that had fought tooth and nail to discredit me and pretend that there wasn't a problem between their police department and black people. Plus, I'd been in several depositions with the District Attorney, the grand jury, and Bill Helfand, the City of Bellaire's civil attorney, and I know how sarcastic and condescending they could be.

With a pat on my shoulder, my dad told me, "See ya in a bit," as though he was going to the ballpark to play a game. He was gone about twenty-five minutes, which was pretty much about how long his depositions had been in the pretrial interviews. The fact is that when the shooting went down, my dad had his face and hands pressed to our Chevy Suburban SUV, with a gun pointed at him, when Cotton came around the front of the truck. My dad didn't get a solid view of what happened because he couldn't turn his head, but he heard everything.

As we'd been warned before, my dad didn't pretend that he'd seen something he hadn't, and that meant that we were able to keep our credibility. Unlike the police officers, I might add.

"This is my son. This is my house. This is my car. We live here," my dad testified. "Two to three seconds later, I heard a bang (of Marian Tolan hitting the garage). A second or two after that I heard a gunshot. Then all I heard was my wife saying 'Call on Jesus. Pray Robbie. Call on the Lord.'"

Anthony was in the room with us, but Greenwood and Morris told us that they weren't going to call him. That hit me hard, and I think it hit him hard. For the most part, during this ordeal, because he wasn't shot, he'd pretty much been ignored.

Years before, Anthony came to live with us when he was a teenager, around fifteen or sixteen, and we instantly saw that he was a good kid with a good heart. Like a lot of families, my parents opened their home to him because they thought that he needed a stable home. Without getting too much into his previous situation, my mom and dad figured that, at such an impressionable age, he needed that special positive attention that could make or break a kid.

I loved having him around because it filled a void in my own life. They say that twins have a sixth sense about the other person who shared a womb with them. Well, my twin died before I was born, and I was the only survivor. Having Anthony in our home felt like a void was being filled. Forget about the cousin versus brother thing, Anthony Cooper, for all intents and purposes, was a Tolan in our house, and that meant that I considered him my little brother, and I'd like to think that he considered me his big brother.

Thoughtful, sensitive, and a person who wears his emotions on his sleeve, Anthony was affected by the shooting as much as I was. In fact, other than the bullet entering my body and not his, I sometimes thought that his mental pain was greater than my physical pain. When I was in the hospital, we never got a chance to talk one-on-one, which is something I'd suggest families allow for if you're in the situation I was in. A one-on-one conversation would have allowed us to sit down and flesh out our trauma, but without that, Anthony just had to deal with the hurt without having a voice. He didn't get a therapist, and he didn't spend his time writing. He just became an afterthought.

We didn't know anything about the type of legal battle we were entering, nor did we have a clue about the severity of the struggle, but the family knew that it wanted Anthony to be involved in every aspect. He'd been there at the shooting, after all. But we didn't really talk to him about what he was going through. From the minute they rushed me to the hospital to save me, the story had been about me, and I think that if I felt trapped, he also felt a bit caged in terms of his feelings. He was in a situation that he could barely make heads or tails of and yet no one was paying attention to him. And just like I wanted to run from the world, Anthony wanted to do the same. So it wasn't surprising that he left our house right after I was released from the hospital and headed to California to live with family friends.

I imagine that Anthony had feelings of emptiness and insignificance, but for practical means, we needed him with us through the criminal and civil trials. The fact that he wasn't there for depositions, or interviews, or a lot of things inevitably drove a wedge between not just him and me, but also between him and my parents. I think my parents looked at his absence as being a bit of a betrayal, in that they'd taken Anthony in when he needed help, and yet when we needed him to be there for us at the weekly press conferences or the several meetings with the attorneys, he wasn't there. No matter what, he wouldn't fly back from California, except for the trial itself.

I don't think Anthony understood that despite the focus being on me as the victim, as a family, we thought of him as being a victim in this situation too. You can't go through something like this and not be harmed, and we knew he was going through the same types of emotions as we were, and in order to get through them, we needed to stay strong as a family. Not just for appearances' sake, but for real.

I could feel that our opponents—the City of Bellaire, the police department, the attorneys for Cotton and Edwards— wanted the Tolan family to be down and defeated, worn down and torn apart by the enormity of the task of finding justice. But we weren't torn apart. We were strong, and I wanted Anthony to see and feel that strength. I knew that if he lived his life feeling that he wasn't in control, such as by not doing something as simple as walking into a room with his adversary and looking them straight in the eye, then he could end up falling down a slippery slope.

I know that sometimes running away feels like the best thing to do, and Lord knows I tried to run. But I wanted Anthony to know that he shouldn't feel guilty about anything and that he didn't have to run away from this traumatic part of his life. Because like anything, if the trauma finds a weakness, or the opponent who caused the trauma sees the weakness, then they can capitalize on it and destroy you. Moreover, you might end up destroying yourself. I don't think that we did a good enough job telling Anthony that he mattered, and I think he felt overlooked and overwhelmed.

There were signs early on that we should have seen. When Anthony gave Bryant Gumbel a tearful and poignant interview during the taping of *Real Sports,* no one ever saw it because it ended up on the cutting room floor. Just before the piece aired, Bryant's producer, David Scott, called Anthony to tell him that he wouldn't be featured in the segment.

"People want to hear about the Tolans, the people who were affected by the incident," Scott reportedly told Anthony.

I don't think Scott meant any harm; he probably just meant that with the limited amount of time for the segment, they only had time to air interviews with my parents and me. But I'm sure the comment cut Anthony, who considered himself to *be* a Tolan and who we considered to be a Tolan, and I think we missed the impact this total process had on him. I honestly think this broke his heart. He'd been asked to give an interview, a cathartic expression that was about telling his story and healing, and then was later told that no one wanted to hear from him. It was a devastating blow to his already withering spirit.

In his interview, Anthony said something that stayed with me. He said that he wished that he had been shot instead of me.

"Robbie is smart and he has so much going for him," Anthony said, fighting back the tears, "and it should have been me and not him getting shot."

I was in the next room watching the monitors and tears ran down my face. This wasn't what I wanted to hear. I didn't want to see my little brother feel so worthless, so without value, that he'd want to sacrifice himself for me. I wanted him to know that he had value and that we loved him. No, I didn't deserve to be shot, but he sure as hell didn't need to think that his life was lesser than mine or that he was expendable. He had the same survivor's guilt that I struggled with after being shot.

It is not hard to understand why, from his vantage point, he felt expendable. All of the early news reports mentioned him being at the scene. But as time went on, he faded from the public eye, and it was just, "the Tolans" this and "the Tolans" that. Media accounts went from mentioning "Robbie Tolan and his cousin Anthony Cooper," to simply mentioning, "Robbie and his cousin." Anthony had been erased, and although I couldn't control that, I hated it.

I seek anonymity, which comes from being exposed constantly to the hot glare of the media's spotlight, but that's my choice as I try to maintain control over my life. But it's different to be erased by others and become invisible, and that's what happened to Anthony. He was standing there, all alone, watching as he became the "other," and it took an emotional toll on him. I thought that Anthony would finally get his chance to speak at the trial, to have his say, and I was hoping that it would be emotionally therapeutic for him. But it wasn't to be.

Next up was my mom, and the same feelings overcame me with her that I had felt with my dad. She was the one I was trying to protect, and my heart raced as she stood up to go to the courtroom. I didn't want my mom to have to walk into a courtroom full of pictures of my bullet-mangled body, because I knew that she'd cry just at the mention of my being shot.

I wasn't the only person dealing with trauma, but my mom did a great job hiding it from the world. But the thought of her crying in front of Cotton and the City of Bellaire was repulsive to me. I get angry just thinking about it because Cotton and Edwards, who were at the trial each day, weren't worth any of the tears my mother shed. I didn't want them to see her as anything but the strong and powerful black woman that she is; I didn't want them to see her as vulnerable to their actions.

Sure enough, my mother came back to the witness room about an hour later, her eyes red from the tears. I tried to be emotionless as she quietly described her emotional roller coaster because I knew I was next up on the stand, and I needed to be emotionally steady. She told them about the various bruises she'd suffered from Cotton as he manhandled her.

"I kept telling them that this was our house and that was our car, but they [Cotton and Edwards] wouldn't listen," Mom told them. It was hard for me to see my mom go through this trauma again, but I thought to myself that I had to use that as motivation.

"Concentrate on being focused and fearless," I repeated to myself. "Concentrate on being focused and fearless."

A few minutes after my mom sat down, my Uncle Charles and Maria came into the room.

"Robbie, they're ready for the star," she said.

I was ready. I was more than ready.

I stood up, put on my jacket, and hugged and kissed my parents. I gave a bro hug to my cousin Anthony and then headed to the elevator. Once the elevator doors closed, Maria turned toward me.

"You're going to first go to an empty waiting room just across from where the trial is being held," she said. I just nodded. I hadn't said a word; I was concentrating on what was going to be the biggest at bat in my life.

As the elevator slowly approached the ground floor, I could hear the now familiar scuffling of the photographers jockeying for position to get the money shot of the guy who'd been shot. When the doors opened, it was madness.

Hundreds of camera shutters snapped at the same time, and I could hear the telltale sound of the photographers' shoes skidding against the cheap courthouse linoleum floor, as they fought over themselves to get the best position to watch me walk to that empty room. I kept my head down and focused on Maria's heels as we walked. That was my own rebellion against everyone wanting a piece of me. I think at that moment I finally understood what some Native Americans say about the camera stealing one's soul. Each photographer, and I'm pretty sure they're good people, was attempting to use his or her camera to capture some essence of my soul. What was I thinking? Did I have fear on my face? Was I nervous? By looking down, I retained my humanity.

Before I walked into the empty room, my Uncle Charles approached me.

"I'll see you inside," he said, pointing to the courtroom where the trial was being held. He went to the left, back to his seat, and I went to the right.

"I'll be back as soon as they tell me that they need you on the stand," Maria said. And like that, I was alone in the room. For a ten-minute period that felt like an eternity, I was alone with all of my fears and trepidations. I just wanted it to be over. Then suddenly, Maria came back into the room.

"Ready?"

I nodded again. I stood up, buttoned my jacket, and followed Maria into the hallway, where the photographers lay in wait. This was the moment they'd been waiting for, the entry into the courtroom. But this time, I hardly noticed them. I was concentrating on the packed courtroom.

When I reached the entrance of the courtroom, I stopped and took it all in. The placed was packed. I had a thousand knots in my stomach and a nervousness I'd never felt on the baseball field, but there was something comforting about seeing every pew in the room filled to capacity with friends, family, and people who were just interested in the case. There were so many people in the room that many of them were squeezed together uncomfortably, their arms and legs pressed together. This was going to be Houston's trial of the year, and apparently, people wanted to see it for themselves.

"Keep focused," I kept saying to myself mentally as I slowly made my way to the front of the court. I searched for Cotton and Edwards because I wanted them to know that I wasn't afraid. I found them, and they stared beyond me. I didn't even see the court registrar approach with his Bible. I placed my hand on it.

"Do you swear by Almighty God that the evidence you give shall be the truth, the whole truth, and nothing but the truth."

"I do."

"Please have a seat, Mr. Tolan," the judge instructed.

As I got comfortable, I scanned the courtroom and saw that my family was taking up two whole rows in the middle of the courtroom, and that made me feel great.

Greenwood was the lead prosecutor for the trial, and he began his line of questioning. We'd built such a good rapport after so many pretrial meetings, so that I felt that I knew what to expect. I recounted every single detail that I'd ever disclosed to anyone, making sure to not self-edit. I would make them tell me when to stop or direct me into another area, but I wasn't going to do that myself. I couldn't forgive myself if I left something out, simply because I thought that it didn't have any importance. However, all the questions asked were questions that the District Attorney's Office, the grand jury, the reporters, and, hell, even Bryant Gumbel had asked before.

During my depositions, Cotton's lawyers always asked about how I got up from the ground before being shot, as though that was the crucial point. Cotton's lawyers would smugly infer that I wasn't being as accurate as they thought I should be. I'd always explained that to get up from the ground required me to use almost a push up maneuver. I mean, I was lying on the ground, so you have to use both of your hands to push off the ground. But according to Cotton, I'd magically levitated to my feet, which not only made me mad, but also made me laugh. Damn, I'd heard about white folks thinking that black people were magical, but we're not *that* magical. But all of that was the preliminaries, and this was the time to actually show the jury what I'd done.

"So when you give us a re-creation of the shooting, it's your best guess of how you were getting up, correct?" Greenwood asked.

"Yes, sir," I said.

"Mr. Tolan," Greenwood continued, "could you do me a favor and come there and show the court how you got up from the ground?"

I got up from the stand and laid on the ground; then I demonstrated how I had pushed myself up. Months after the trial, I read the transcripts, and Cotton had testified that I'd used his magical levitation method to keep my hands free to "dig in my waistband" as I rushed toward him. It was a bunch of bullshit, and he knew it. And the jury should have known it.

"I pushed myself to my knees, said, 'Get your hands off my mom,' and then he shot me," I testified. "It all happened so fast."

I didn't notice any change in the jury's reaction to my demonstration. They studiously took notes and, I'm assuming, weighed the testimony of Cotton against mine. I made sure that I did the demonstration in the same manner as I had done during our practices, knowing that I couldn't really mess up. There was no way that it took five seconds for me to get up. No way.

For the rest of the testimony, I followed Greenwood's lead. The questions were easy to answer, sometimes only requiring a one- or two-word answer. But he did want me to be as visual as possible, to paint the scene for the jury. It's hard to remember that although I'd been living and reliving this nightmare ever since that bullet entered my body, most people had only heard cursory details via the media coverage. That meant they'd gotten bits and pieces, along with Cotton's and the City of Bellaire's skewed version. So I took particular care to let the jury know where I was, where my mom was, where my cousin Anthony was, and where my dad was, in relation to where I was. And most importantly, I indicated where Cotton and Edwards were. Every single miniscule detail up until the shot was fired was treated like a precious jewel. Then Greenwood posed a question that struck me silent for a full minute.

"What went through your brain when you were shot?"

The courtroom held their collective breaths. I know it's a cliché to say that you could hear a pin drop, but before I responded, seriously, you could have.

"I was gasping for air. I couldn't do anything. I blinked and I was on the ground."

"What happened next?"

I remembered this like it had happened yesterday, even as I felt like that elephant on my chest from the bullet collapsing my lung was going to crush me.

"Cotton came over to me and was kind of on my left shoulder

like this," I continued, showing where Cotton was standing. "He then pushed me on my back and asked me what I was reaching for, all while he was digging in my pockets."

"What were you reaching for?" Greenwood asked, not looking at me but at the jury as he asked the question.

"I wasn't reaching for anything."

"Did you have a gun on you?"

"No."

"And did you charge him?"

"No."

All of my testimony was in direct contrast with what Cotton had said on the stand. I knew right then that the jury was going to need to make a black or white decision, metaphorically of course, about whom to believe. It was going to be either me or Cotton.

Greenwood then went to the prosecutor's table and picked up a handful of pictures.

"Let me approach, your honor, and show you what has previously been marked State's evidence 120, 121, and 126." The judge nodded and Greenwood brought the photos to me. "Do you recognize these photos?"

"Yes, sir," I said. The photos were pictures of my chest wound.

"Do they fairly and accurately portray the bullet wound in your chest?"

I could feel the emotion welling up in my chest. My physical wounds had healed, but they were always there.

"Yes," I said, choking up. Remember I said that I didn't want Cotton and Edwards to see my mom cry? Well I sure as hell didn't want them to see tears running down my face either, so whenever I felt vulnerable, I turned to those two rows of pews filled with friends and relatives who loved me unconditionally. But then I made sure to look directly at Cotton. I wanted to look him directly in the eye as a sort of "Fuck you, I'm still here," but he wouldn't look at me during my entire stint on the witness stand. I would make eye contact with him for a split second and then he'd quickly shift his eyes downward. But I didn't care. With each pause in the direct examination, I'd stare at him. I wanted him to be as uncomfortable as possible, to have to figure out different ways to turn his direction away from me and toward fumbling with the notes he had in front of him. And I wanted the jury to see how his conscience wouldn't allow him to see me.

"I have no further questions, your honor," Greenwood said. When I heard that, my whole body tensed up as I braced myself for the questions from the defense attorneys. They were going to try to do their best to discredit me, to make it seem as though I was responsible for getting myself shot. I needed to be prepared and ready.

Mr. Paul Aman, the leading litigating attorney, sat quietly at the defense table. In earlier interviews, he'd stated that, "Sgt. Cotton acted as a reasonable police officer would have acted under the circumstances." It might seem like a reasonable action to the uninterested people in the public, and when I say uninterested, I mean anyone who didn't take a bullet to the chest. But it wasn't a reasonable action from my perspective. And that's what we were going to litigate in the trial.

Sitting next to Mr. Aman at the defense table was Dale Paschal, a guy who was a spitting image of Santa Claus, with his long white beard. I'm not saying this to disparage him; he really did look like Santa Claus. Paschal led the cross examination for the defense team, and I was a bit leery because I had heard that the defense team had a tendency to be condescending to everyone on my side, so I wanted to make sure that I didn't fall into any traps.

It was a bit of a game, and I knew that Paschal had to tread lightly when questioning me. One way to turn a jury against the police was to seem like you had to beat up the victim of the shooting in order to prove your point. So the defense attempted to present a case that wouldn't necessarily make me unsympathetic, but instead, just a tad bit liable for getting shot. That way, they wouldn't appear inhumane while attempting to get Cotton off. But I was ready for them.

As much as it cut me to the core that they were defending Cotton, I made sure that I remained nice and polite to them. I was polite to a fault. When they asked a question, I began the answer with a sir and ended it with a sir. The jury needed to view me as the polite kid I was, and not their stereotype, so I was polite more for their sake than for the defense.

I was also encouraged by the fact that it seemed like the judge was much more on our side than the defense's side. We knew that judges tend to favor prosecutors, at least according to Geoff's early prediction, but we were going against a police officer, so I thought that getting an even shake would be a tall task. However, the judge was consistently sustaining the objections of Greenwood, while overruling most of the objections of the defense team. I'm no lawyer, so I'm not sure if the quantity of objections sustained or overruled has any bearing on how a case is going, but it seemed to me that the prosecution was winning the case in a landslide.

In preparation for the case, I'd been advised to take my time while answering questions from the defense. I'd been taught to listen attentively to every sentence, as the defense might try to trap me in some type of rhetorical word play that would make me admit to something I didn't understand. So instead of just rattling off a series of quick answers, I'd pause for a couple of seconds and think clearly before answering. That seemed to rattle the defense, which must have thought I'd get on the stand, become emotional, and lose my cool. Nah, I wasn't about that life while on the witness stand.

Paschal seemed to become increasingly frustrated at my answers and the calmness with which I gave them, and I think that colored his last two questions to me.

"Mr. Tolan," he said, his brow furrowed, "is it true that you and your family have a civil case pending against Mr. Cotton and the City of Bellaire?"

"Yes, sir."

"Well, Mr. Tolan, don't you think it helps your chances of seeing some sort of monetary compensation in the civil case if Jeff Cotton is found guilty?"

I took my customary few seconds before answering.

"Well, I'm not exactly sure, sir. I'm not an attorney."

The whole courtroom laughed, including the judge. Paschal retreated back to his seat behind the defense table and plopped down. After fumbling through his notes, he rested his head on his right hand.

"I...I have no further questions, your Honor," he said resignedly.

The judge turned to me. "Mr. Tolan, you're free to leave."

As I stepped down from the witness stand, I spotted Maria, who was to escort me out of the courtroom. It was cool to see my pastor, Kirbyjon Caldwell of the Windsor Village United Methodist Church, squeezed in the last row. As I was about to leave, he extending his fist and bumped it with mine.

"Outstanding job," he whispered.

It felt good. And then the courtroom doors opened again, and the cameras exploded. Maria and I rushed to the elevator doors, waiting an eternity for the doors to open as the photographers took shot after shot. Finally, they opened, and we quickly got inside. Just as the doors were about to close, one photographer shouted from the back.

"Robbie, how do you feel right now?"

"I'm just glad that it's over...for me anyway."

# CHAPTER 6

## JUSTICE FOR ALL?

**Eric Garner, 43, New York, New York—July 17, 2014**

Eric Garner, a forty-three-year-old African American father of six and grandfather of three, was killed in Staten Island, New York, after NYPD officer Daniel Pantaleo subdued him using a banned chokehold. Garner, who had previously complained in federal court that an NYPD officer had once conducted a search of him by "digging his fingers in my rectum in the middle of the street," was allegedly selling loose cigarettes when arrested. Recorded on a cell phone video, Garner can be heard saying, "I can't breathe" before losing consciousness and dying. Although the New York Medical Examiners ruled Garner's death a homicide, a grand jury refused to indict Officer Daniel Pantaleo.

W|ell, we just rested," Greenwood said, as he met us back in the witness room. "The ball is now in the defense's court."

Greenwood and Morris had done a great job presenting the case and had made the strategic decision of not calling my cousin Anthony to the witness stand. The goal was to puzzle the defense and throw a wrench into their case.

"They won't know why we didn't call on Anthony, and it'll confuse the hell out of them," Greenwood explained. They also explained that they thought we had a really strong position and that everything was tilted in our favor. But even though we'd all testified, we were still not allowed to watch the trial, because the defense could possibly call us to testify again.

As the trial continued with the defense making their case, I left each evening with my dad and headed over to Bellaire High School, where we created our own version of spring training, as I tried to get in shape for Dmitri's team in Detroit. One consequence of the trial was that my shot back to baseball was delayed until there was a verdict. The training wasn't optimal, but it was something. I wanted to be somewhat prepared when I finally joined the team.

Back in the courtroom, Greenwood and Morris had predicted that the defense wouldn't put on a long case. They might even rest on the first day back, and then both the prosecutor and defense would present their closing arguments, and we would have a verdict in a day or two. And that's exactly what happened. The defense rested after only two days.

The defense brought forth Monica Barron, a Bellaire police dispatcher, who said that it appeared that after I'd been shot Cotton had gotten impatient with the Emergency Medical Services, or EMS, because "it appeared EMS was not getting there fast enough for them."

Yeah, I'd be nervous about a citizen dying too if I knew that my actions, which were all wrong, had led to the shooting.

Cotton's former supervisor on the Bellaire police force, Zell Woods, testified that Cotton had always been truthful, but I took that with a grain of salt. The Thin Blue Line tended to vouch for each other; otherwise, you would be blackballed by other police officers. I could just imagine Woods going, "Yeah, I always thought that Cotton was a liar," and then seeing thousands of cops descending on the courtroom. I'm not saying that Woods was lying, but let's just say that I'm pretty sure that he gave Cotton a lotta rope when it came to the idea of being truthful.

"Closing arguments will be tomorrow, and the rule about you being in the courtroom has been lifted," Greenwood informed us. That meant that we could finally go to the trial and see the ending. Also, the prosecutors were now free to tell us what happened while we were sequestered in the witness room.

We were so anxious to hear the intimate details of the trial that we all grabbed chairs and took notes, like Greenwood and Morris were old sages about to tell us a legendary tale. And with my relatives now coming into the room, we were all exchanging our own perspectives about how various aspects of the trial went.

We quickly identified a few holes in the defense case, and we could clearly see that Cotton and Edwards had changed their stories. In his testimony, Edwards had stated that my cousin Anthony and I were both screaming at him as he approached and that he couldn't make out exactly what we were saying. But in another part of his testimony, Edwards suddenly remembered very clearly what he thought we were saying. According to him, when he approached us and ordered us to the ground, with a gun pointed at us, he said, "Yeah, they kept saying 'Fuck you, fuck you! We don't have to do what you say!'"

All right, let me stop right there. Now remember, we're in our own driveway, staring down the barrel of a gun while being blinded by a flashlight...at two in the morning...in a country that has been shooting black men left and right. What part of that scenario would make a rational black man think, "Sure, this just might be the time to pop off at a police officer." Nah. But I could clearly see that they were trying to play off the stereotype of the angry black man, times two.

Plus, here's another thing about being black. You know how you talk. What do I mean? You may not know it, understand it, or even believe it, but there's a cultural way that black people create their sentences and the rhythm of the sentences to the point where it's like a fingerprint. You can call it Ebonics; linguists called it AAVE, or African American Vernacular English, a dialect of English. It's English, but with a certain cadence and wordplay that's unique. You can't approximate it, but you can stereotype it.

Months after the trial, I sat across the table from Edwards in a civil disposition, and he again said that we had told him, "Fuck you, fuck you! We don't have to do what you say!" and he was as unconvincing as I thought he'd be. Not only was it not true, but it also wasn't authentic. It's a white person trying to say what they *think* a black man would say under the circumstances. It's using the racism within white supremacy to tap directly into how other white people see people like me, a young black man who isn't the polite young gentlemen in the witness stand, but a belligerent menacing thug who has no respect for authority, is a constant danger to police, and caused his near death by mouthing off when he should have been following orders.

Now I didn't get a chance to see Edwards at the trial, but again, at later depositions for the civil case, there was one thing that bugged the shit out of me. He was arrogant as hell. You'd think that a man whose irresponsible, lazy, and sloppy mistake caused another man to nearly lose his life would have an element of humility in his manner. You would think that, even though he wasn't the one charged, he'd look at me with some sort of contrition or maybe just an acknowledgment that if he could do things differently he would have double-checked my license plate.

But there wasn't an iota of humanity in him that I could see. And if I look at it from his perspective, why should he feel contrite? The Bellaire Police Department didn't reprimand him or hold him accountable in the least. As far as he was concerned, he didn't do anything wrong. So when he recounted his memory of what we said, he delivered it like a man who thought he was invincible.

On the other hand, I had to give it to Cotton. The shooting and trial seemed to have humbled him. If it wasn't for him fabricating details of the shooting, I might have had a bit of sympathy and compassion for him. But just like Edwards, Cotton fumbled over his words and testimony, which led Greenwood and Morris to declare him a bad witness.

But let's go back. Trying to understand Cotton's mentality from the jump is what makes me mad, in that it was his brazen decisions that set off the series of dominos that left me with a hole in my chest. Because the Bellaire Police Department had put its officers on a hair trigger because of their search for auto theft suspects, Cotton had unholstered his gun when he got out of his police car because he thought we were dangerous criminals, even though Anthony and I were on the ground with our hands in plain sight.

"I drew my weapon and ran up to officer Edwards. This is a felony arrest. It would be normal to hold suspects at gunpoint," Cotton said on the stand. The defense then played a videotape of Cotton saying that me being on the ground was a good thing.

"He was on the ground and everything was going to be sorted out without deadly force."

Then Cotton, who, if you remember, burst onto the scene without announcing himself, said that he didn't realize that the older woman standing on the doorstep at two o'clock in the morning was my mother, even though he admitted that she identified herself as "the homeowner."

"She was doing a lot of talking, and not a lot of listening," Cotton said. Again, that pissed me off—this notion that this police officer, along with Edwards, who had collectively done no listening to any of the black people at the scene, would then assume that we were supposed to listen to him. Remember, we had done nothing wrong. My cousin and I were lying on the ground, my dad was standing up against the Suburban with a gun pointed at his head, and my mom was being harassed *in front of our own home and next to our own cars,* and yet not one of these guys stopped and listened to us. They just assumed we were at fault based on a mistake. So color me skeptical when I heard that Cotton suddenly was concerned about my mom.

"I was taking her to the garage for her own safety," Cotton said. "I heard him yell. I turned and looked as he was getting up. I pushed her, took a step away from her, faced him and drew my weapon."

Now stop right here. What do I mean when I say Cotton fabricated details of the shooting? Well, during the pretrial investigation, he said that I had something shiny in my hand, but at the criminal trial, suddenly I was doing something else.

"In front of this jury today, you've testified that Robbie Tolan was digging in his waistband, correct?" Greenwood asked.

"That's correct," Cotton said.

"Have you ever said anything different?"

"Well," Cotton said, hesitating, "I may have characterized it differently, like reaching into his waistband or something like that."

Greenwood decided to press Cotton because it was important

to show the contradiction between what Cotton had said before and what he was saying during the trial.

"Have you ever made the statement, he was digging or reaching into his pocket?"

"No. Not that I recall."

"Have you ever made the statement to anyone that Robbie Tolan had something shiny in his hand when you shot him?"

"Absolutely not. No."

That's when Greenwood knew that he'd gotten Cotton because of his previous testimony.

"That would be a lie, wouldn't it?"

"Yes it would be a lie."

In my eyes, it was all a lie. I didn't reach for my waistband, I didn't have anything shiny in my hand, and I didn't I yell out "Fuck you, fuck you!" It was all made up, and Greenwood said that later on in the trial, he'd gotten Cotton to disavow the idea that he'd seen me either "digging" or "reaching" into my waistband. His new testimony was that my hand was at the center of my body or in the vicinity of my waist and that he wasn't even sure that he could actually see my hand because my "clothing was probably covering it up." Cotton also said that a tree was casting a shadow on the front porch where I was, and that he only had one option, which was to shoot first and ask questions later.

"We're trained that if you wait until you see the weapon before you react, you will get shot," said Cotton. "I thought he was going to shoot me."

Wait, you mean to tell me that police officers can shoot you simply because they think you have a weapon? Maybe that's why an officer killed Castile when he was pulling out a wallet instead of the firearm he *warned* the police officer he was carrying.

"I couldn't believe he was getting up. I kept thinking to myself, don't do it, don't do it," Cotton said in a pretrial videotape that was played in court. "I thought he was drawing a gun."

And that's basically how it broke down. I was shot because a guy came running onto the scene with a loaded gun, but didn't make a correct assessment of the situation, and then compounded that mistake by misinterpreting what I was doing, while admittedly not seeing clearly. And for that, I'm supposed to feel sorry for him that he felt bad for me.

Look, none of us—not the lawyers, the police, my parents, or I—disagreed that I yelled, "Get your fucking hands off my mom!" And I don't regret protesting the mistreatment of my mother, not one bit. But I do sometimes wonder if a different exclamation by me would have resulted in a different reaction from Cotton. At the very least, should I have perhaps avoided using profanity? Still, that does not justify deadly force any more than profanity toward a policeman hints at imminent violence.

I looked it up, and the court ruled in the 2012 case of *Morris v. Noe* that a suspect asking, "Why was you talking to Mama that way?" was "potentially confrontational," but not an "overt threat." In *Bauer v. Norris* (a deputy Sherriff), a court ruled that "the use of any force by officers simply because a suspect is argumentative, contentious or vituperative is not to be condoned."

I want to think that Cotton, if he was given truth serum, would agree with the court cases, because he did sound contrite when asked about his reaction to learning that this whole ordeal had been one big mistake.

"Officer Edwards came over to me and told me the car was not stolen," Cotton said, "and my heart dropped."

Cotton then described what happened after he'd shot me.

"I watched him long enough to figure out that he's not a threat anymore at this point. So at that point I moved forward. I holster my weapon and I start checking him for weapons. I'm looking for the gun. When I can't find the gun and I search and search his pockets. I search his waistband. I searched underneath him, no weapon...he was just groaning. He was obviously in pain. I said a prayer for him because at this point when I couldn't find the gun, I was just hoping that he was going to live."

Hoping that I was going to live. That's what I was dealing with after all of the bad judgment. Hope.

"I checked for wounds," Cotton continued. "I found the entrance wound on his chest and I was kind of—I checked him for an exit wound and couldn't find one and I—I was confused as to why there was only one wound because I knew I had fired more than one round and I couldn't find any other wounds in him. And so I checked him even more extensively and still couldn't find—I checked his legs, still couldn't find any."

I asked my relatives about their reaction to listening to Cotton's testimony, and each one of them said it made them very emotional. Again, that's the toll that comes from being even tangentially connected to a shooting victim of the police. But there was something else I was interested in: Did Cotton seem contrite? Did he seem like he had remorse? From the info I gathered, it seemed like he did have some remorse, but I wasn't in the courtroom to see it myself.

It's hard to talk about all of this without also acknowledging that despite the effect this shooting had on me, I'm still a human being who is bound and determined to not be bitter and hateful. Jeffrey Cotton is a man. Edwards is a man. And I'm sure that they have families who love them and who they love back. I'm not trying to be heartless in how I see them, and I know that Cotton was facing a possible ninety-nine-year sentence for shooting me. I get it; it's serious, and his life was basically on the line. But what about me and what about my life and the ramifications of their mistake that I'll have to live with for the rest of my life? I didn't want to see either of these men destroyed, but they had basically destroyed part of my life.

Did I want either of them to go to jail for the rest of their lives? No. But I didn't understand how two people entrusted with the responsibility of serving and protecting the public could make a nearly fatal mistake, with me dodging death only by the grace of God, and still keep their job. Accountability and losing their jobs were the punishments I wanted for Cotton and also Edwards, whose incompetence led to me being shot. I didn't think that was unreasonable or revengeful. It was simply the best outcome for all of us, mainly because both Edwards and Cotton had revealed that in the heat of the tough job of police work, neither was capable of making good decisions. That in itself should be a permanent disqualifier for wearing the badge and holding life and death authority over other human beings.

The trial lasted six days, and most of my family had used hard-earned vacation time to be in the courtroom, even when they knew I couldn't be there. That's what family love is all about, and I wanted to repay them by sitting right there with them during the closing arguments. So on that day, we arrived early, with even more family coming in droves to hear how Greenwood and Morris would put the cherry on top of our case.

We took up much of the center section of the courtroom, and I sat in the front row in between my mom and Pastor Caldwell. The butterflies in my stomach danced around as though I was giving the closing arguments myself. When Greenwood and Morris entered the courtroom, each was carrying stacks of books and notes.

"Looking forward to making this closing argument," Greenwood told us, as he greeted the family. "Just wanted to make some final touches to my speech to the jury."

The prosecutors Greenwood and Morris had done everything that we'd asked of them up to that point, and my family had been happy to have them on our team. Having experienced a shooting by a person operating under the color of the government, we weren't necessarily the most trusting of people when it came to believing that the prosecution had our best interest in mind. But our initial skepticism was tempered by our faith in God. Our faith had gotten us to the indictment and then finally to the trial. We put our faith in Him, and He gave us Greenwood and Morris. It was now in His hands.

My relatives had glowing reviews of Greenwood's work in the courtroom. Other than during my own testimony, I hadn't seen him in action, so I was excited to see what he could do with his closing argument. I wasn't disappointed. In short, Greenwood delivered a poignant and powerful closing argument that left me confident and impressed. He noted that Cotton had come up with three different versions of why he'd shot me, including saying that I'd been carrying something shiny, which he then later recanted.

"An unarmed kid was shot by the Bellaire police, and you know what? He wasn't doing anything illegal," Greenwood told the jury. "It's a tragedy of errors, not a comedy of errors, a tragedy."

Of course, the defense wasn't as impressed as I was. In their closing argument, Aman and Paschal somehow decide that I wasn't the victim in this case, but *Cotton* was. Yes, the person who rushed to the scene, gun drawn, and shot me in the chest was the real victim in this saga. As the defense team went through their arguments, they colored me as a delinquent menace that was just looking to get into a fight with police. The fact that I was unarmed while the two policemen had loaded guns pointed at me was just an incidental fact, apparently, to the defense. I was the dangerous one—the one on the ground with his hands up.

Having to silently listen to the defense tell lie after lie was probably one of the hardest parts of the trial. I couldn't say anything because the bailiff would escort me out if I did. What was worse was hearing the defense play on the ugly racial stereotypes that my racist email and letter writers sustained themselves on. I said that the guy who sent me the death threat would find his ideas in the courtroom, and there they were.

Objectively, though, Aman's closing arguments in contrast to Greenwood's were dull and mediocre. I thought we were winning on all fronts, and the prosecution did too. They felt very confident in our chances for a conviction as we broke for lunch after the arguments.

"Go get some lunch, relax in the witness room because we have no idea as to how long these deliberations will last," Greenwood told us. "But you will be given ample notice before you have to return to court."

Okay, I thought, let's head out. With my family in tow, we took a back entrance out of the courtroom and headed to the Spaghetti Factory in downtown Houston and relaxed a bit. I didn't talk too much but allowed myself to enjoy the presence of my family. After about an hour, we headed back to the witness room, where everything seemed pretty normal. Some in my family decided to sit around and talk about various aspects of the trial, while others passed the time by playing cards. I walked around the room, looking at my family, and realized that we could have been at any other family gathering, but this was a tad bit different. I still had the weight of the verdict on my mind, and although Greenwood had warned me to not expect an immediate verdict, I couldn't get it out of my mind that a jury was now discussing me. I sat by the window by myself and looked out over the city of Houston, as I tried to relax and clear my mind. Amid the laughter and conversation, I almost didn't notice that the witness room phone had rung.

The phone ringing wasn't really a surprise, as the attendant typically answered it a bunch of times during the day. Sometimes the calls were to tell us that we could go to lunch, other times that the attorneys wanted to meet with us, so I didn't pay attention. But then, the room got deathly quiet. My dad called for me in a soft voice.

"Robbie, the jury has a verdict."

The room instantly became chaotic, as everyone fumbled

to gather their things. We had about forty minutes to get to the courtroom, so technically there was no rush, but you know how an expectant father gets flustered and runs around like a chicken with his head cut off when his wife is in labor? That was the fifty or so relatives in the witness room. Plus, we all wanted to make sure that we sat together in the courtroom, so we wanted to get into the pews quickly.

My heart was pounding as though my freedom was at stake, instead of Cotton's. By now, the witness room wasn't as secret as it had been at the start of the trial, and when we walked into the hallway toward the elevator, a lone reporter pretended to wander aimlessly around, waiting for me. My family formed a big circle around me to keep the reporter from me, as I really wasn't in the mood to answer any more questions. I think he got the message, and he just let us walk to the elevator without a word. My heart pounded as the elevators slowly descended to the ground floor and the waiting courtroom.

When we finally reached our stop, the elevator doors opened to pandemonium. Dozens of reporters bombarded the doors, and as we got off, my family did their best to circle me again. Other relatives had taken other elevators and added their bodies to the big circle as we slowly made our way through the crowd of reporters and photographers. As I looked at the chaotic scene, I could see nothing but the arms and hands of reporters and photographers trying to reach over my family to get a shot of me or maybe a statement.

Inside the courtroom, I spotted my relatives seated in the first three rows. I sat in the front row between my parents, pretending that I was calm and collected. I pulled out my phone and fiddled with it, but I could hear the chatter from the people around me. It was like they were betting on the outcome, with some positive and others pessimistic.

Greenwood and Morris walked in confidently and greeted us. They noted that after the verdict was read, they would escort us across the hall to the witness room opposite the courtroom.

"We feel really good about a conviction," Morris said before he and Greenwood took their seats behind the prosecutor's desk. Cotton and his lawyers took their places behind their desk, and soon after, the courtroom doors were flung open and the bailiff walked in with the jury. Two of the jury's nine women were black, and the rest of the jury members were white men.

"All rise," the bailiff commanded. We all stood as the judge finally entered the courtroom. The judge sat behind her bench and began thumbing through some papers.

"There will not be any outbursts from anyone after the verdict is read," the judge said with a stern voice. She encouraged everyone to exercise their best poker face, but in a trial this emotional, I knew that was going to be a Herculean task for it not to be an outburst either way. It felt like my heart was racing a thousand miles a minute as the judge explained to the jury that when she asked him to, the foreman would stand up and read the verdict. It was just like you see on shows like *Law & Order*.

"Has the jury come to a verdict?"

The foreman, who seemed just as nervous as Cotton, jumped up and said, "Yes, your honor."

And then it happened.

"We, the jury, find the defendant, Jeffrey Wayne Cotton, not guilty."

From that moment on, as the foreman's words flowed over his lips, I did not hear another word. Not from the judge. Not from my relatives who surrounded me, shouting and crying despite the admonitions of the judge. Not from my parents who squeezed my arm. My heart had dropped, and I felt paralyzed. My eyes glazed over, and people said that I had a blank expression on my face, to the point of spacing out.

"Come on, Robbie," my dad said quietly, grasping my arm. The rest of the courtroom began to empty, with Cotton being congratulated by his defense team. People around me were standing up to leave, but just like when I'd been shot, my brain couldn't comprehend what had happened. Surely this wasn't the real verdict, right? This had to be a bad dream that I couldn't wake myself up from, but if someone pinched me, I'd wake from this nightmare, right?

I stood up and looked around to find almost everyone staring back at me. I mustered just enough strength to get my weak legs to start walking toward the door. Every step was painful, affirming my nightmare. I felt like there was a bottle of champagne inside me that had been shaken profusely and was ready to explode. I was able to keep my composure during the short walk across the hall to the empty courtroom.

Cameras and reporters were everywhere, but I didn't give a damn. Greenwood and Morris held the courtroom door open for me and my family to enter, and I walked past Greenwood, barely seeing him. I started to unbutton my jacket as I walked past Morris, and without even realizing what I was doing, I slid the jacket off my shoulders, then down my back and arms, and then slammed the jacket onto the ground.

"You've gotta be fucking kidding me!" I screamed at the top of my lungs.

"Robbie, no!" Morris said, running over to me, but also looking back at the open door to the witness room where the reporters and photographers were still shooting pictures. He didn't want to give the media any ammunition, but at that point, if you can please excuse my French, I didn't give a fuck. Yeah, looking back, perhaps I should have reacted differently, but at the time, I didn't care what the media said about me. That champagne bottle of emotions had been opened and was exploding everywhere. I thought then, and I still think now, that I was justified in being upset because it was the wrong verdict.

Greenwood and Morris hurried the rest of the family into the room, as they tried to do damage control, but it was too late. That night, and for the next several nights, "You've gotta be fucking kidding me!" was plastered on every television and every newspaper.

"Robbie, you can't do that," Greenwood said. "You can't go off like that, even though we lost."

"This is his life," Morris said in my defense. "You've gotta understand that."

I didn't hear anyone as I collapsed to the ground, clutching myself as I curled into a ball. "I cannot believe this," I cried out. "He was even eligible for fucking probation and he got nothing? Absolutely nothing? You're kidding me, right?"

Not only had Cotton been acquitted of aggravated assault, but also of the lesser charges of assault, deadly conduct, and reckless endangerment. They didn't convict him of anything.

Meanwhile, Paul Aman was outside talking with reporters, completely triumphant.

"We are very happy with the verdict," said the defense lawyer, Paul Aman. "We believe we presented a good case, and Jeff was never guilty of these charges."

Sergeant Cotton said, "I'm glad it's over. I just want to go back to work."

My body went limp. Several family members surrounded me and tried their best to console me, but I was completely and utterly devastated. My loud cries became near silent guttural moans. I could hear everyone expressing their disgust and disbelief, and I was drowning in the prayers of two long-time family friends, who were on each side of me, hugging me and whispering prayers into my ears. I'd never been so stricken with grief in my life, and in some ways, it was like being shot in the chest all over again, but instead of an elephant being on my chest, the weight of the universe was on my shoulders.

"When he fell, it was like he'd been assaulted again," Marian remembered. "It was a deep, deep pain. We didn't even know how we were going to get him out of the building."

Greenwood and Morris apologized profusely for the verdict, as they'd truly been convinced that they would win. They had tried hundreds of cases against police officers, and Greenwood thought this was one of his best cases in terms of clear-cut evidence, but then, nothing. My family didn't think they had anything to be sorry about. To a person, my family and I thought that they'd done a fantastic job, but it was the jury who didn't do their job. And I needed answers about why they didn't do it.

"Guys, I'll be right back," Greenwood said, as he excused himself. "I want to see if I can speak to the jury."

It is the right of the prosecutor, and reporters for that matter, to see if jury members can give them a little insight into the deliberations. Because it only took a few hours for my jury to come to a not guilty verdict, I didn't think that they'd really given the evidence the consideration that it required. But as Greenwood went off, I got up and sat in a chair, limp and lifeless. I felt like my heart was going to implode.

"Is there any way that we can get out of here without the reporters seeing us?" my mom asked Morris. "I need to take my baby out of this courthouse."

"Absolutely," Morris said. "Just give me a bit of time."

After about thirty minutes, my family had calmed me down enough so that I could stand up on my own. I held the wall up for the next several minutes trying to think about anything other than what had just happened. I knew I would have to leave at some point so I straightened myself up and put my jacket back on in an attempt to get myself together. By that time, Greenwood had re-entered the room.

"Well, not only did they not want to speak to me," Greenwood said in disbelief, "but they asked to be escorted out of the building."

That was enough for me. I needed to get the fuck out of that courthouse. Greenwood and Morris led us out of the witness room and through the empty courtroom to a door that led to a long white hallway. We were told that the reporters were still hanging by the elevators, so we had to take a back way to our cars in the parking garage. When we got to our cars, I said goodbye to as many of my family members as I could because I really did appreciate their support. They'd proven how much they loved me. Others made plans to meet us in Missouri City at my Aunt Carolyn's house, just so we wouldn't be alone through this.

On the way home to my Aunt Carolyn's, I don't think I spoke a single word. Not one single word. And no one bothered to talk to me either. My mom and aunts were hysterically replaying all of the inconsistencies within the trial—where the defense hadn't proven their point, where Cotton had lied, where Edwards had lied—and they were in utter disbelief at the outcome. It had rocked their world as much as mine. Meanwhile, I sat in the car numb. I could feel my phone vibrating from all of the calls, text messages, and Facebook and Twitter posts from people expressing their anger and sadness at the verdict, but I couldn't look at them yet. All I wanted to do was get into the house and be alone.

As soon as we arrived home, I leapt out of the car, opened the door to the house, and fled to the solace of my bedroom. The only thing I did was take off my shoes before sitting up straight on my bed with my legs crossed, damn near the same position I was in during those days right after my release from the hospital when I was dealing with nightmares and night sweats. I sat there in the dark, lights off, and let everyone else congregate in the living room while I was alone with my thoughts. I could hear them talk about the trial, but I didn't listen to what they were saying. I didn't care. I just stared at my feet in complete darkness, alone in a depression that was trying to consume me, and I wasn't resisting.

If you're reading this and thinking I'm being overly dramatic, do me a favor and imagine someone in your family being nearly murdered because of a mistake. Take the police officer out of the equation, and just imagine another human being deciding that they were going to shoot your mother, your father, your aunt, uncle, son, or daughter in the chest, and as a result, your neighbors were going to have to make a judgment about whether or not that was right, and they came back saying, "Yeah, even though it was a preventable mistake that caused all of this, you still deserved that bullet." You'd be beyond pissed to the point of going to a dark place as a result of your lack of belief in humanity. That's where I was. I had a bullet in my body, and the police officer who'd put it there said that he couldn't wait to get back to work.

I needed something to snap me out of this. Something to show me that staying in this darkness—and I'm not just talking about the darkness of my bedroom—was not good for me. I needed light, and I needed hope. I couldn't change what happened in the criminal case, but I needed something to make me want to wake up in the morning. As I sat in that bed, I felt like I was going to die. I could really see myself committing suicide. Why? Because society had said that my life wasn't worth shit. Just as with hundreds of other black people who'd been shot and sometimes killed by the police, juries around the country had simply shrugged at our plight. So why the hell would I want to walk this earth that unprotected? But then I remembered that I did have something to live for.

Baseball.

And I needed that little game of balls, bases, and bats more than ever.

# CHAPTER 7

# A BLACK LIFE NOT MATTERING

### John Crawford III, 22, Beavercreek, Ohio—August 5, 2014

John Crawford, a twenty-two-year-old man, was purchasing a toy BB rifle inside a Walmart when a white shopper, Ronald Ritchie, called 911 and claimed that Crawford was waving the gun and pointing it at customers. Store video would later show that Crawford wasn't pointing the gun but, instead, was on the phone with the toy in his hand. Within seconds of arriving, the police shot and killed Crawford after claiming that he didn't comply with their orders to lie on the ground. Being that Ohio is an open carry state, Crawford would have had the right to carry a real rifle in public, which prompted an argument over whether blacks are afforded the same rights as whites when it comes to carrying weapons in public. A grand jury declined to indict the officers who killed Crawford.

My eyes began adjusting to the darkness, and as they did, I began to see things around my room. The closet. The wall. The pictures on the wall. It was like my brain was trying to force light into me, despite my despair. And as such, I began thinking, not about the jury's verdict, but about the light at the end of the very dark tunnel. I started thinking about baseball, and it was just then that my Aunt Carolyn and mom entered my room and asked if I wanted to leave for Detroit. I'd forgotten. Detroit was where spring training was happening, and I'd already missed a week.

"I don't care about baseball," I told them, but that wasn't true. I did care about it. I didn't care about hitting a baseball or making the major leagues, but I did care about baseball as an escape. I'd previously told Dmitri that I'd fly out to spring training the day after the verdict, and when I checked my phone, I saw that I'd received calls and text messages from him asking about the verdict and what time I'd be arriving.

"Not guilty," I texted him back. "I'll let you know when I head out to Detroit later."

Luckily, I wasn't alone in this decision. Remember when I said my mom was a fighter? She wasn't going to let me wallow in my darkness; she was going to get my behind into action. While I was in my room and my extended relatives were gradually leaving, she found and booked a flight to Detroit for me. I was going to leave the next morning, and it was for my own good.

Just before my parents left, I started to pack. They promised to come back in the morning to take me to the airport. I texted Dmitri to let him know that I was on my way, and he texted me back to say that he personally would pick me up from the airport. A little later, Aunt Carolyn and Uncle Charles went to bed, and again, I was alone with my thoughts. But now, I didn't want to hide from the world. I needed to express what I was feeling to the world. Where were all of those reporters and photographers now? Who wanted to hear my unfiltered voice, and who would be brave enough to publish it?

I rushed over to my bag, pulled out a small black notebook, and began to write furiously. I hadn't fully processed my thoughts, but that didn't matter. I didn't care about making sense; I just wanted to vomit out the emotions from my brain to the pen and paper. This is what I wrote:

I am extremely disappointed in the citizens of Harris County, Texas. Out of sixty-four potential jurors for the case, twelve were selected that were supposed to be the best representation of the people within the county. Twelve jurors were selected that were supposed to be unbiased, untainted, and undecided. These twelve pur-portedly competent people chose to side with injustice.

I cannot imagine that the members of the jury who had children felt this was the right verdict. None of these men and women remotely made an attempt to put them-selves in the shoes of the people who were involved. In Texas, a notoriously prejudiced state, I believe people will always have a problem convicting a white police officer for shooting a black man, always; no matter what the cir-cumstances. White people hate when we play the race card; granted, it's not something I like to do, or even make a habit of doing, but wrong is wrong.

I have never been one to attribute my successes and failures to race having been a factor. After the verdict was read, my family and I were forced to keep our poker faces as instructed by the judge. I looked over at twelve people who seemed to have their minds made up from the open-ing arguments of the trial. I looked at twelve people who looked at dozens of pictures of bullet holes in my parents' roof and in my chest, staples in my stomach, and bruises on my mother's arm, police logs with lines blacked out to hide something, and listened to audio tapes of me ago-nizing in pain, and my mother crying and praying for her son as police officers told her to be quiet and that she was not allowed to pray; every one of them looked abso-lutely ashamed. None of them would look anywhere in our direction; they all looked down or purposely in the opposite direction. All it took was one courageous person to speak out against injustice. Just one!

The judge gave the prosecutor, Clint Greenwood, an opportunity to speak to the jury behind closed doors; an opportunity Clint jumped at. The jury declined to speak with him, and asked to be escorted out of the building immediately. I cannot for the life of me understand their logic; those twelve jurors sat through five days of the trial and listened to all of the evidence. They heard all of the holes and inconsistencies from the defense and their testimonies, then came back with a verdict that was supposedly appropriate, and just. If they stood by their decision, why lower their heads in shame? Why refuse to speak with Clint? Why ask to immediately be escorted out of the building? I might have at least respected some of them if they had appeared vaguely confident in their decision, but I witnessed the indignity on their faces.

As a police officer, Cotton was even eligible for probation had he been convicted; he got absolutely nothing but a fifteen-month vacation. The facts of the case were as clear as day. My life was threatened; hanging by a small string. I had to leave the game I loved; piling up medical bills and attorneys' fees in the four hundred thousand dollar range. Meanwhile, Jeff Cotton maintained his full salary and benefits during his administrative leave; and was also given his job back.

Police are always going to get the benefit of the doubt in Texas; I am okay with that. As I got older, I gained a far better understanding of the dynamics and unspoken protocol for existing as a black man in such a red state like Texas. So I am okay with giving them the benefit of the doubt; what I am not okay with, is when all of the facts are staring you in the face, and you make a conscious choice to look away. Those twelve jurors, that were supposed to represent the people of the progressive major city of Houston, have no integrity. This case was supposed to send powerful reverberations throughout the city, communities, and police departments. It was the perfect opportunity to begin to hold policemen accountable for their actions. The verdict was a terrible message to send to the community and our youth.

I have maintained one position throughout this entire ordeal, and that position is: I do not hate police officers. I was taught to respect and trust in them to do what is right. Just like any other profession, there are good officers, and bad officers. Police officers have a tough job, and they should be recognized for it. But since we expect so much of them, we should also hold them to a higher standard than we do ourselves. We impeach presidents and congressmen for lying about affairs and falsifying documents; why shouldn't we hold policemen to the same standard?

Policemen are the people we trust to protect us when we are in danger; where was my protection on December 31, 2008? My protection tried to kill me. Now who am I to trust and call when I am in trouble? Am I to take matters into my own hands? Of course not. I would be wrong if I did that, right? Who am I to trust? I wished those twelve cowards understood there are laws designed to hold public servants accountable for their actions, if you enforce them. When President Barack Obama elected Eric Holder as the Attorney General, he came out of the gates swinging with a very bold statement that has stuck with me and holds true during moments such as this verdict:

"We are a nation of cowards."

I kept that small black notebook with me for two years without looking back at these words, but I knew that the raw emotion in my rant was a true reflection of how I was feeling at the time. For years after the verdict, I let the jury's decision eat me alive because I just couldn't make sense of it. What were they looking at that made them come to this decision? Was being a police officer such a powerful position that you could completely exonerate a man for making a nearly fatal mistake? Now, I will never look at jury summons the same. Back in the day, I used to look at a jury summons with the same annoyance that most Americans do, with one thought in mind: How in the hell do I get out of it? Not anymore, my friends, not anymore.

By virtue of my experience, I now recognize that jury duty is a privilege. Yeah, it can be an exasperating process, but when I think about the people who could have served on my own jury, who could have brought a different thought process, I believe the verdict could have been different. And I'm quite sure that many Houstonians who were upset by my verdict are some of same people who resist the notion of serving on a jury due to the inconvenience.

I've spent countless sleepless nights wondering whether some of the people who sent me letters of support after the *Real Sports* segment had decided to not serve on the jury when summoned.

Or did someone who asked, "Is there anything I can do?" on a Facebook post say no to their civic duty? Did all of the people who could have spoken up indeed speak up?

As a victim, I pray that everyone who serves on a jury takes the time to learn to empathize with the victim in the trial. I mentioned how I thought the hardest thing for a jury judging a black man shot by a white cop was going to be the empathy factor, and I was right. The jury in my case had the chance to do something right, and they didn't. I'm sure that if the shoe were on the other foot, they would want someone to stand up for justice for their son or daughter. And for that, I unapologetically call them cowards.

I've come to the cynical conclusion that most people are inherently selfish. Yeah, this is a dark view of humanity, but I find that people are mostly just interested in talking about making a difference, but not actually doing what that requires. And I think that if you dive deep into the frustrations that drive black people, including all of us who support Black Lives Matter, it's that we want people to stand up and make a difference. Listen to me. See me. Hear me. Don't just fall for the notion that society is safer if a police officer is allowed to shoot and kill without repercussions. What message does that send to our sons and daughters?

Returning to that reporter's question I mentioned earlier, about what you tell a black kid like me about believing in the system, I'd have to reiterate that I don't know what to tell that kid. Again. Remember, for a second, I had hope. We have dozens of campaigns encouraging kids to vote, to remain abstinent, to say no to drugs, and to do a plethora of other things, but what are we telling them about being empathetic to other human beings?

What do you stand for in life? If anything, this experience has taught me to stand up for those whose voices get lost among the powerful. I count Greenwood among those who stand up.

The day after the verdict, my mom received a call from Greenwood, who was very upset.

"Marian, I tried...and I'm sorry. I really tried," he said, his voice solemn. "I just don't know what happened. We had a really good case against him."

I always felt that Greenwood was genuine. He didn't have to call my mom, but he did. That's what you do when you see people as being human and you can empathize with them. I knew that he knew that Cotton was wrong, and although I only saw Greenwood in trial action, I trusted him.

Near the end of the conversation with my mom, Greenwood said that he'd contacted the FBI to potentially try Cotton at the federal level for violating my civil rights.

"Marian, I sent them everything," Greenwood said. "All of the notes, the pictures, the videos, transcripts, I sent it all." He was hopeful that one way or another, Cotton would be held responsible for his actions.

In the end, that's all I wanted to happen. I don't hate police officers, but I do want them held accountable. But just as I see that people are loath to empathize with other human beings as victims, I'm starting to see that accountability isn't an important attribute in America when it comes to victims with black skin.

Now before you get all up in arms, know that I don't believe in being prejudiced against any race, gender, or profession based on the wrongdoings of one person. Edwards and Cotton are not like every white police officer. I know that. And growing up, my parents never even talked about the contentious relationship between white police officers and black people. My parents raised me to have a strong moral foundation that centered on the Golden Rule from the Bible: "Do unto others as you would have them do unto you." I was taught to respect everyone, no matter who they are, including police officers. But now, things are different.

I know that police officers don't care if I'm polite. I know that police officers don't give a damn if I own my car. I know that police officers don't give two shits if they're actually on my property. I know that police officers don't care for me. And I can't help but think that it's because of the color of my skin.

After the verdict, I had dozens of police officers, black and white, approach me and express their discontent with the verdict. And I had a lot of civilians say the same thing, and I always thought, "Then why don't you do something to change the system? Stop saying that police officers have a tough job or that we have to believe in the system." Here's my call to action for America: Do something to change the system.

All of this was on my mind when I got on the plane to Detroit. Besides being in the worst emotional state of my life, deflated from the outcome of the trial, I again felt guilty for being the center of the emotional world of my family and then, the next day, leaving their lives. Yes, I was excited about getting back onto the baseball field, but it felt like a dark cloud had descended not only over me, but also over my entire family, who were all devastated by the words "not guilty."

Was I running away from my problems or chasing my dreams? Was I standing up for my mom or getting ready to attack a police officer? Like everything in life, it was complicated. My parents, the two most important people in my life, were left to pick up the pieces. I felt like I should be there to be as strong as they were for me.

I thought about how often I had run when they had stayed. I'd run from my old house on Woodstock, while they crossed the same threshold where I'd been shot each and every day. In some ways, I had run away from baseball, but my dad had stayed with it, bringing me back to the B.A.T. convention so that I could find myself on this plane going to a new team. I ran away from the media, the reporters, and the interviews, while my mom stayed to fight for me. However, my parents are not invincible, and even though they have the support of my family, the strength of their religion, and just good old stubbornness, I'm sure their quiet moments are not only stressful, but also heartbreaking.

The early morning ride to the airport was somber, and my melancholy mood didn't help matters. It was my true emotion, the depression that comes from having one's hopes and dreams dashed, but as my parents kept telling me, "Life goes on."

"We're proud of you, son," my dad said, "and you're going to have a great season."

With every word, more and more tears filled my eyes. These people loved me so much, and I loved them. As I kissed them and we said our goodbyes, I put the hoodie over my head and strode through the airport hoping to not be recognized. But as I looked around, I felt like I was in a scene from *The Twilight Zone;* everyone in the airport was reading the front page of the *Houston Chronicle,* featuring none other than me. I made eye contact with one man and watched as he looked at me, then at the newspaper, and then back and me. Yeah, that was gonna be my life in

Houston and that meant one thing: I needed to get the hell out of Houston.

When I landed in Detroit, the team had been in spring training for a week, which meant that I had to get my mind right and my body right at the same time. It was cold and raining or, as some of the players said, "Welcome to Detroit" weather.

Let's be frank; the Frontier League isn't the big leagues by any means, and that means that the money was funny and the owners weren't giving out a lot of it. Most players stayed with host families, but I was lucky. I stayed with Dmitri at his business manager's house, Dave Bailey, with another ball player, Kris Kararjian, a guy from just north of Los Angeles, who went to UCLA. I loved staying there because I was comfortable, we all got along, and it felt like a family.

Let me stop here for a second and explain why I'm talking about my time playing baseball. I'm not telling you about it because I think you share the same undying love for the game of baseball. I am relating this part of my story for one reason: baseball pretty much saved my life. Remember when I talked about using writing as a way to heal myself mentally versus going to a therapist? Well baseball played the same role in my life. Heading to the baseball field while running around and chasing and hitting a baseball was therapeutic for me, and I didn't know I needed this therapy until I started it.

When we weren't at practice, the three of us spent a lot of time just chilling—watching TV, playing Xbox, and watching endless movies on DVDs. The evenings were spent eating at a local restaurant called Outriggers, and we generally just had a great time.

One day after practice, I had a candid conversation with Bailey, who told me that, as for making the team, I basically had a "free pass." I asked him what that meant, and he explained that once it was agreed that Dmitri was to join the team, Dmitri requested that I come too. The owner of the team, Rob Hilliard, had to be convinced though.

"Rob, don't you think the kid has been through enough?" Bailey asked, lobbying on my behalf. "Plus, it just might bring some good publicity to the team having Tolan on it."

Being a smart businessman, Hilliard agreed that me being on the team would be a good thing, if I was willing to give interviews. And you know, I was grateful for the opportunity, so if the *Houston Chronicle* or those *June Bug*–type newspapers my mom used to talk to needed an interview on chasing my dreams, then boom, I was going to give it to them.

"Initially when it happened [being shot], I never thought I would be in a uniform again, and as soon as I heard the doctor say I should make a full recovery, the first thing that was on my mind was baseball from that point on. I was determined to get back to this point," I told the reporters.

I didn't feel as much pressure to perform knowing that I didn't have to worry about making the team. But, for me, just making the club wasn't enough. I wanted to start. That was the one way to pay back Dmitri, Bailey, and Hilliard for giving me a chance.

However, like everything in my life, the road toward my goals wasn't exactly straight. The curve was that it turned out our owner was supposed to build a new stadium. That was the good news. The bad news was that it didn't happen, I heard, because the necessary paperwork wasn't submitted to the city to obtain the construction permit. This was unfortunate, especially if you were a player or a coach who liked playing half your games within driving distance of your house. Instead, it meant that the team would spend the majority of the ninety-six-game season on the road, while playing only eighteen home games at Eastern Michigan University.

You don't have to be a genius to understand what that meant. And if you've ever seen a baseball movie about the minor leagues, you know that even in the best of times traveling is dodgy. It's all bus rides, bad food, and cheap motels. Now imagine that you're on the road endlessly. It's going to affect your performance. But, ironically, it didn't affect mine.

I loved playing on the road, meeting different people, and seeing different towns. I was thrilled when I got a chance to play the Evansville Otters at Bosse Field, the third oldest stadium in the country, only surpassed by the Boston Red Sox's Fenway Park, and the Chicago Cubs' famed Wrigley Field. It's where the movie *A League of Their Own* was filmed. So that part was dope.

Despite everything, we had a lot of talented players on the team, and we were playing very well. I started off on fire; I was hitting over .300 and was seeing regular playing time. I was getting back to being me. Ah, but it seems my life wouldn't be complete without some type of tension. It turns out that the general manager and Dmitri, who was now the hitting coach, didn't get along, even though we were in first place. In a power struggle, the general manager began releasing players left and right, but I still remained.

Eventually, our team entered a downward spiral during the

second half of the season, and a full-blown revolt was close to happening. Baseball players tend to be paranoid, especially when they see good players being released. It makes them nervous.

The slide was gradual. First we relinquished first place, and then the avalanche came; soon we were out of playoff contention, and the club lost the revenue that came with being in the playoffs. Members of the club began to show up to more and more games, interfering with us during batting practice and before and after games.

Then there was some mysterious tax that came out of our game checks, something to do with a fine the league had imposed on the club but that the players were paying. Still, we had fought back to get to the last game, which we eventually lost. Our season was over, but I was as happy as if we'd won.

In the clubhouse, everyone was giving little goodbye speeches.

"I really loved playing with you all ...."

"I think I made twenty-five different friends, and not just teammates ...."

That sort of thing. When you're on a team, sometimes you play with people who you can't wait to get away from, even in the major leagues. There is a famous quote about the Red Sox being "twenty-five players taking twenty-five cabs," meaning that these players weren't a team, but individuals. But our clubhouse felt like a team, despite the hurdles of playing mostly on the road, players being dropped left and right, and our losses. In the midst of these little speeches, Dmitri turned to me and mouthed the words, "Say something."

I'm an introvert, not a person who seeks the spotlight. You may have noticed that, during my whole ordeal, I sought the background, hiding when possible. So I told Dmitri, quietly and to the side, that I didn't have anything to say. But as the speeches went on, Dmitri whispered in my ear.

"I really think you should say something. I think the team really needs to hear from you."

And then, after a brief pause, Dmitri blurted out, "Hey Robbie, aren't you going to say something?"

And there I was, right there in the spotlight. I gave a nervous chuckle of embarrassment for having been put on the spot, but Dmitri had given me this chance to play baseball in the first place. He'd given me months of thinking about nothing but a game; he game me the opportunity to not be in Houston, having to worry about the civil case that Geoff Berg was busy preparing. In short, he'd allowed me to clear my brain, and now I needed to use that clear brain to think of something to say to people who'd helped save my life.

Everyone was watching me, and my mind was moving a million miles per hour.

"Look, I just want to thank you all for being great teammates," I started. "You helped me escape a very tough time in my life and I'm forever appreciative. I'm a living testament to the grace of God, and no matter what happens on the field, or off the field, we're all blessed to play this game. Of course, we all want to do well, and we want to win, but at the end of the day, it's just a game. A kid's game. Don't take it too seriously. Enjoy it."

I was surprised by the reaction to my speech. They all seemed to be moved, with each one of them giving me a hug afterward. We all got together for one last meal, and then it was off to our respective homes. For me, heading back home to Houston was bittersweet. I was revitalized, but now I had to stare my continued struggle in the face. We'd lost the criminal trial, but it was now time to fight Cotton in the civil courts. Things wouldn't go smoothly, though, and to quote the famous title of Nigerian author Chinua Achebe's best-selling book, *Things Fall Apart;* elements of my life would resemble that title.

# CHAPTER 8

# RENEWING THE GOOD FIGHT

**Michael Brown, 18, Ferguson, Missouri—August 9, 2014**

Michael Brown, an eighteen-year-old resident of Ferguson, Missouri, a suburb of St. Louis, was shot and killed in the middle of the street by Ferguson police officer Darren Wilson. Brown had allegedly robbed a convenience store earlier; however, Officer Wilson had initially stopped Brown for jaywalking. Wilson would end up shooting Brown in the middle of the street, where Brown would lay dead for hours, leading to weeks of unrest in Ferguson. Officer Wilson was not indicted by a grand jury.

Once the criminal trial was over, the civil trial was next, with the Bergs leading our case. As disappointing and devastating as the criminal verdict was, we still had to realize that the odds of us even getting to trial had been long, and the strategy had been to sue the two Bellaire policemen and the Belleaire Police Department anyway. However, we started having issues with our legal team because they seemed to lose their enthusiasm for our case.

Nearly two years earlier, they had walked into my hospital room and given me the impression that we had a "slam dunk" case against the officers, but now, suddenly, we were hearing things like "The odds are looking less in our favor" and "Our chances don't look good." Whereas Geoff Berg and his legal team had previously seemed certain that we could press the City of Bellaire and the Bellaire Police Department for full compensation for our pain and suffering, the Bergs were now saying that "We might want to settle so we can get something out of this."

"I want to be honest with you," Geoff Berg told us, "so that you don't get your hopes up."

In our private family meetings, we agreed that being realistic is one thing, but being pessimistic is another thing altogether. My mom had been very clear from the start that she was not interested in settling. She didn't like the idea that you could shoot a young black man and then pay off that man for pennies on the dollar. She wanted the officers to feel the pain so that they'd think twice about doing it again in the future. We also thought that our legal team were scared that they weren't going to see a return on their investment, and that put us at loggerheads. They wanted money as fast as possible, in our eyes, and we wanted justice.

"The City of Bellaire and the attorneys for the officers are very interested in settling, but they want us to initiate a proposal," the lawyers told us. So we did.

In our first settlement proposal, we called for the City of Bellaire to implement new policies regarding diversifying the police department. We also wanted a public apology from the city and the police department, along with the resignations of Sgt. Cotton and Officer Edwards.

As for money, Berg asked for an eight-figure amount for me and six figures for my parents and Anthony. And then we gave them a deadline to respond. They ignored us. According to our lawyers, they didn't respond because we asked for too much money. That meant we were headed to court. And this is when things began to get worse for us.

Before you start thinking I'm just some greedy schmuck

who is looking to make money from being shot, it's important to put the dollar amounts in perspective. In the Houston area alone, there had been a bunch of settlements from various police departments.

In the city of Webster, an entrepreneur sued four officers alleging false arrest. He settled for $62,500. The parents of a mentally ill patient who was killed by Houston area cops were given a $150,000 settlement.

Settlements reached nationally included the following. The relatives of Freddie Gray, a twenty-five-year-old man who sustained a fatal spinal cord injury, reached a $6.4 million settlement. The family of Kenneth Smith, a twenty-year-old hip-hop artist who was fatally shot in 2012 by an off-duty officer, was awarded $5.5 million. New York reached a $5.9 million settlement with the estate of forty-three-year-old Eric Garner, who died in 2014 after police used an illegal chokehold.

So I wasn't out of line thinking that if we were going to settle, not having died shouldn't work against me when it came to the amount of money the City of Bellaire would pay. This was about making the money amount to a punishment for the City of Bellaire for not having the foresight to protect its citizens from racial profiling, because when taxpayers have to pay, they pay attention.

But the City of Bellaire's thinking was quite different. Instead of firing Jeffrey Cotton, they decided to promote him from sergeant to lieutenant. I mean, for what? Shooting me? Being a ten-year veteran who'd ruined the life of one of its citizens? His promotion spit in my face and the face of my family, and I was more determined than ever to make the City of Bellaire and the Bellaire Police Department understand that they weren't just going to walk away from this by doing what they'd always done, which was to ignore the problem of racial profiling and ultimately reward their officers.

Our case landed on the desk of U.S. District Court Judge Melinda Harmon, and if you were looking for someone to advocate for the civil rights of citizens over the police, then this was a worst-case scenario, at least according to our lawyers. They told us she had a reputation of throwing out just about every single civil rights case she ever received.

Judge Harmon had spent most of her time working either for corporations as a trial lawyer, such as for Exxon, or as a judge in district court overseeing cases like the Arthur Anderson obstruction of justice case regarding their officials shredding papers concerning the bankrupt and defunct Enron. She'd gained notoriety by setting legal precedent in this case by ruling that jurors could reach a verdict on the company as a whole, even though they failed to agree on the individual responsible for ordering the shredding.

According to an interview she did with BBC News, Judge Harmon noted that she agonized over the ruling because "I'm kind of in a position of a case of first impression, which is terrifying for a district judge," she said, aware that her ruling could set a precedent and be subject to future legal challenges.

Little did Judge Harmon and our family know that this wouldn't be the only case that would set a legal precedent in her courtroom.

But still, we were a bit encouraged when Judge Harmon ordered us to engage in a settlement conference with a magistrate judge, which made Geoff happy. He thought that Judge Harmon could have simply thrown out the case.

Unlike how prepared we were when the Harris County district attorneys Greenwood and Morris worked with us for weeks before the trial, my family and I didn't feel as prepared for the settlement conference. When my parents, Anthony, and I arrived for the initial conference, there were ten people from the City of Bellaire sitting on one side of the table and just us and our lawyers on the other side. I think the city was trying to intimidate us, but I made sure that I walked into the room and eyeballed each one of their representatives.

We sat across from each other until the magistrate judge arrived, and she escorted us into two jury rooms in the back of the courthouse, with the city in one room and us in the other. As the mediator, the judge was to have us go back and forth with our proposals until, at least theoretically, we came to a settlement. Of course, the City of Bellaire and the police department wanted us to go first. So we made our proposal. But then the judge left the room before we could hear the counterproposal from the city.

With the judge gone for what felt like an eternity, I became impatient and increasingly annoyed by being in the same room with people I'd grown to disdain.

"Geoff," I whispered to Geoff Berg, as we waited, "if they come back and counter with some bullshit proposal, then I'm leaving."

Geoff's eyes got big, and he took me to the side. "You can't do that, Robbie. You can't leave before the judge is satisfied that we gave a good faith effort to reach a settlement."

"Well, then," I said, not wanting to compromise, "they better not come back with something ridiculous, or I'm serious. I'm out of here."

"You just can't leave a settlement conference," Geoff reiterated. "You just can't do it."

"Oh for real? We can't leave? Watch me!" I said, ending the discussion. At that moment, the judge walked back into the room, and we retook our seats.

When the judge came back into the room, we held our breaths as she read back the city's offer.

"Their counteroffer was two hundred and fifty thousand dollars," she said.

I looked at Geoff and then back at the judge. I was incredulous. "Well, your honor," I started, "with all due respect, but we came down half of what we originally asked for. I have well over two hundred thousand dollars in medical bills, not to even talk about my attorney fees. I'm close to four hundred thousand in debt, and that would come off the top of any settlement I'd receive, and they know this. To be shot by them, and then be repeatedly denied a simple apology, and then you come back and offer only two hundred thousand dollars for my troubles? That's a slap in the face. And your honor, I refuse to go back and forth playing their game all day, so my family and I are going to leave."

"Okay," the judge said. And with that, we walked out, to the astonishment of our lawyers. I think, at that moment, our lawyers began to think we were a lost cause as clients.

For weeks after our walkout, the lawyers kept encouraging us to settle the case, or I might not receive anything. I was okay with that. If we were going to settle, I told them, we were going to settle on my terms, and no one else's. It was frustrating, though, because we were feeling pressure both from our lawyers, who were trying to sway us to take pennies on the dollar just so we'd stay in debt, and from wanting to beat the city. But in all honesty, I think the seeds of the split between my family and the lawyers had started during the criminal trial.

Geoff had attended several days of the criminal trial, but the communication between us started to wane. What was once a biweekly check-in was reduced to a quarterly email, if that.

I think my lawyers, who saw me in the hospital, didn't get the essential reason for my fervor. They couldn't wrap their heads around the idea that my case wasn't about the money, but about my life. This incident, which was beyond my control, put a pause on my life that I could never get back, no matter how much I rehabbed, worked out, or mentally overcame it. I didn't want to settle for what would have been a throwaway amount. If I did that, my voice would have been gone.

After we walked out, there were no more talks about settling with the city. Now we were playing a waiting game over who would blink first. But before we could deal with the city, we had to have a heart-to-heart with our attorneys.

My parents set up a conference call with David and Geoff, my main attorneys, and again, they gave us their best sales pitch to try to get us to settle. After listening for about thirty minutes, I'd had enough.

"I'm really freaking disappointed," I said, pissed off.

"Why?" David asked, truly surprised and confused as to why I wasn't happy. That pissed me off even more.

"When you guys first came to visit me in the hospital, my

mother asked if you were ready to fight for us. And you know what you said? You told her yes. Then, visit after visit, you continued to come into my room, with my family, and go on and on about how good a case we had, and that Cotton and the City of Bellaire were going down! You were all gung-ho. But now, now that it gets a bit tough, and you all want us to just take any kind of bullshit that they throw at us? This is my life, guys. I've been fighting my whole life, and I refuse to fight against people who claim to be on my side."

"Look Robbie, you've got to understand...."

At that point, I wasn't interested in hearing what they had to say. This had gone on for months, and it was clear that they didn't care about what we wanted. So I spoke directly to my parents.

"I'm done," I said, shouting at the phone. "Mom. Dad. You all can call me back later on if you want to, but I'm done. I'm getting off the phone now."

After that conference call, the emails stopped, and any contact we had with the lawyers' office was done through their assistants. The wedge grew wider, but the civil case was moving forward regardless. That meant more depositions for my parents and Anthony, held at the law offices of Berg & Androphy, while I came in later because I was out of town.

The City of Bellaire had hired Bill Helfand and Norman Giles with the legal firm of Chamberlain Hrdlicka, and Helfand conducted my parents' deposition. George Gibson, the one attorney with whom we'd had the least amount of face time, monitored him. I wasn't there, but my mom said that the deposition got heated, to the point where Helfand, who apparently is very skilled at rattling people's nerves, asked my mom several condescending questions such as, "Did you even graduate from high school?" But through it, she stood firm and strong.

Then came my time in front of the lawyers. My dad and mom and Anthony accompanied me to the deposition, and although they didn't tell me who was going to be there from the law firm, I figured that since I was the star witness Geoff Berg would be overseeing everything—you know, just to make sure I didn't fall into any legal word traps Helfand was trying to spring on me. But when I got to the law office, in walked a short bald guy who I'd never seen before.

"Hello," he said, as I reluctantly shook his hand. "Geoff couldn't make it unfortunately," he explained, "but I've read up on the case, so I'm pretty familiar with it."

Wait, what? I thought to myself. You guys want to settle this damn thing to the point of sending some guy we haven't met in two years? Not a single person from our so-called super team of attorneys showed up for my deposition or Anthony's. I was pretty disgusted and irate, but there wasn't much I could do about it. As always, my goal was not to be frazzled by the City of Bellaire, Cotton, or the police department. Like the British say, I needed to "Keep Calm and Carry On." I accepted the circumstances and tried my best to compose myself.

The deposition itself was relatively easy. All I had to do was tell the truth, the same thing I'd been doing throughout this ordeal, so it was extremely easy to keep my story straight. The questions asked of me were no different from what the Harris County DA's office had asked, what was asked at the trial, or what was asked during the dozens of interviews I'd given. But my attorney proved to be very little or no help.

I'm no lawyer, but it appeared that when I needed my lawyer to speak up, he was getting steamrolled by Helfand. Every time he voiced an objection, he stumbled and fumbled when asked to state the legal objection. It was like it was the first time he'd thought about the question, and it was embarrassing. Even though I handled the questions just fine, I think the city felt that it had the momentum because they appeared to be more unified and competent than my team.

Now, I was already irate, but something that happened during one of our several breaks really pissed me off. During the breaks, each side would go to a break room for privacy and confer with their attorneys. Our break room was on the second floor, and near the end of one our breaks, we heard a knock on the door.

"Hey guys, how's it going?"

It was Geoff Berg. Not only was Geoff in the building during our deposition, but he had the gumption to walk in on our meeting like nothing was wrong, like he hadn't made time to be there himself. My blood began to boil, and my parents could see it. I expected him to defend me, not to pop in to see "how it's going."

I walked by Geoff as though he didn't exist, while my dad tried to make small talk in order to lower the tension. As I stood by the stairs, my mom came over and I guess my face did a bad job of disguising my disgust.

"I know," she said without me saying a word.

My dad joined us, and as we walked up the stairs toward the conference room where the deposition was being conducted, standing outside the conference room door was Helfand, who represented the city, and Joel Androphy, the partner in Berg &

Androphy, the law firm that was representing me, yucking it up as though they were best friends.

Sure, Androphy wasn't representing us technically or legally, but his legal partners were, and I thought this was a huge conflict of interest—not legally maybe, but perception-wise for your clients, the Tolans. And no, I can't hold it against the two men if they have a prior relationship and a good rapport, let me say that it wasn't a good look.

So when I saw this, a thousand thoughts ran through my mind. I even started to wonder if the two sides had an under-the-table deal that we didn't know about. I started thinking that that would explain why our attorneys were so adamant about trying to settle for such a small amount of money. Every time we had told the lawyers we weren't interested in settling, they'd had a clear look of disgust on their faces. At the end of the day, I realized that their desire to settle had other motivations, including their recognition that we, and they too, could ultimately end up with nothing.

What they didn't know is that I didn't care about the case being thrown out. They were predicting that scenario, but then again, they predicted that we'd never get an indictment from the Harris County DA's Office, and how did that work out? But more importantly, I didn't give a damn about being left with nothing if the case was thrown out. Making the City of Bellaire pay a fair amount and having Cotton and Edwards apologize was about me having my voice heard. Being broke with a lot of bills? Not my main worry; I'd been broke before, I would be broke again, and I was broke now. But the one thing this private introvert has never been is quiet. It may take some effort to pull it out of me, but when I do speak, I own that voice. Having Bellaire pay was that voice speaking loudly. In any event, my conclusion was that Berg & Androphy had lost confidence in the case and they wanted out.

I don't blame the lawyers for wanting to take care of themselves. My main problem with the lawyers is that they made us think they were better than that when they walked into my hospital room and convinced my family members, who were at their most vulnerable, that they were genuinely concerned about fighting for justice.

After the depositions, we endured more months of waiting, and by then, my family wanted to be rid of the firm, and based on the firm's lack of contact with us, I'm sure the feeling was mutual. I needed people who would fight, who would show up at a deposition and represent their client and not send one of their coworkers.

One day, I looked at my phone and saw that I'd missed a call from Geoff, which I knew was important because we hadn't heard from him in months. He left a message on my voicemail, but it was pretty vague. But only a few minutes later, my mom called in a panic.

"Hey, did you talk to Geoff?"

"No, I just got the call. What's up?"

"The judge threw out our civil case and has ordered us to pay the officers' court costs," she said.

"What?" I was incredulous. Yeah, I knew it was possible the case would be thrown out, but to also have to pay the court costs? That was the literal definition of adding insult to injury. So when

I got off the phone with my mom, I immediately called Geoff to see what was happening and why it happened.

"Judge Harmon determined that Cotton and Edwards were protected by qualified immunity, so she dismissed the case," Geoff said, genuinely sounding distraught from the news.

Judge Harmon wrote the following in her ruling: "Under the doctrine of qualified immunity, public officials, such as police officers, acting within the scope of their authority are shielded from liability for civil damages insofar as their conduct does not violate clearly established statutory or constitutional law."

Judge Harmon ruled that she believed that Cotton feared for his life and did what any reasonable officer would have done in the same situation. Call me a bit skeptical, but what is reasonable to one officer may be bad training to another. And in the case of my shooting, you almost have to assume that the reasonability bar had been set as low as possible.

According to Jody Armour, a professor at the University of Southern California Law School, "all these [police shooting] cases turn on how reasonable the perception was that a black young man posed an imminent threat of harm. That's always the question."

"We're not appellate attorneys," Geoff said. "But I can have my assistant compile a list of appellate attorneys who could possibly handle any appeal that you'd like to file."

A few days later, I got another call from Geoff. His voice was sober, almost humbled.

"What's up?" I asked him.

"Just wanted to call you myself and tell you that I left Berg & Androphy," Geoff said.

Whoa, I thought. I had issues with the firm and its lawyers, but I never thought Geoff would leave his firm.

"We were just going in different directions," he said. He told me that he was thinking about either starting a new firm or joining an established one. I know it was a hard choice to leave his father, but that wasn't why Geoff was calling.

"Uh, since the case was thrown out, I'm sure that my dad and George will withdraw from your case. So if you win your appeal, you'll have to find other representation."

And with that, we were officially done with Berg & Androphy, but really, it had been clear for months that they were no longer the lawyers for us. We didn't want to settle, and they did, and when this notice came, I'm pretty sure they thought that they'd been justified. I don't think the fact that the case was thrown out disturbed them at all, except for the fact that they wouldn't get anything now that we weren't getting anything.

But soon, my human instincts kicked in. Despite our contentious relationship, I wished Geoff and the others well. I don't think me and my family were unreasonable in demanding the type of representation that we deserved. After all, lawyers are called advocates for a reason, and we wanted Geoff and his firm to advocate for us without fear or pessimism.

About a month later, exactly what Geoff had predicted came true. Dave Berg got me and my family on a conference call, and he told us what he thought was bad news but, to us, was great news. Berg & Androphy had dropped us as a client. I'd gotten what I wanted, and I couldn't have been more pleased. A few days later, we received what I thought of as a Christmas gift, a certified letter from Berg & Androphy that read:

Dear Tolan Family and Mr. Cooper:

I wanted to confirm in writing our discussion this morning. Geoff and I have informed you that we are not proceeding in your case. I understand that Martin Siegel is filing the brief on appeal. I neglected to tell you that Nathan Sommers Jacobs [the firm that George Gibson is with] is also withdrawing and they asked me to convey that message. Call me with any questions.

Our firm considers it an honor to have represented you in this matter and, of course, hope that you prevail in the Fifth Circuit.

Sincerely,
David Berg

An honor. Yeah, thanks. After the judgment, Geoff sent us an email:

As you know, the judge awarded Cotton and Edwards the costs of court as part of their summary judgment (attached). That is an expense of $6,755.54 payable jointly by all of you to Cotton and Edwards. We will file an opposition to the award of costs, but because they are awarded as a matter of routine, we are not likely to succeed.

I was glad to be done with the Bergs. I watched as Geoff did interviews. I'd basically gone to radio silence with the reporters, so they went to the next best thing. On camera, Geoff did appear to be disappointed in the judgment, but there was no pretense that he had ever shared our faith in how things would precede, essentially saying, "Well, yeah, this is what we expected."

Now that the case had been thrown out, we had only thirty days to find an appellate attorney and file an appeal. Geoff sent over the list, and one attorney he raved over was a man named Martin Siegel, a Harvard Law graduate and classmate of President Barack Obama. So we scheduled an appointment to meet Siegel.

My research on Siegel, even before we met him, told me that he was the type of lawyer we had needed all along. He was a lawyer who had experience fighting for the little guy. He had successfully represented small taxi companies against the city of Houston with the opinion described as "one of ten of the most important issued by the court in 2011." He had defeated the Republican Party and supported the right to vote against repressive voter ID laws. He was a fighter, and we needed a fighter, not someone who represented us with one arm tied behind their back because they didn't believe we could win.

On this trip, my mom, Aunt Carolyn, and Pastor Kirbyjon Caldwell joined me around a round table with Martin Siegel in downtown Houston, and the meeting went well. Before we even agreed to let him represent us, Siegel sounded like he already represented us.

Siegel said things like, "Once I file our appeal…," instead of "If you hire me, I will begin working on your appeal…," which is what we probably would have heard from other lawyers.

He was a breath of fresh air because he answered every question with confidence. Even though he spoke as though he was rushing to get the words out, his diction was one of conviction.

Most importantly, Siegel didn't appear to be timid, and he didn't seem to think we were going into a losing battle.

"We weren't very happy with our former attorneys," I told him. I wanted to be straight up. We then detailed all of the things that dissatisfied us about Berg and his legal team, and Siegel seemed understanding and sensitive to our concerns. At the end of our meeting, the decision to hire Siegel was unanimous, and he began working on our appeal immediately.

Game on.

# CHAPTER 9

# HISTORY AND THE SUPREME COURT

**Tamir Rice, 12, Cleveland, Ohio—November 22, 2014**
Tamir Rice, a twelve-year-old African American
boy, was playing with a BB gun at a Cleveland park
when Cleveland police officer Tim Loehmann shot
and killed him less than two seconds after arriving
at the scene. Officer Loehmann was not indicted by
the grand jury. Officer Loehmann had previously
worked as an officer in a Cleveland suburb police
department, where he had been deemed emotionally
unstable and unfit for duty.

To get our case back on track, we had to appeal it to the Fifth Circuit Court of Appeals in New Orleans, Louisiana. Three judges from the court were selected to hear our case, and instead of allowing us to address the court, Siegel told us that the attorneys would have only twenty minutes to present their arguments. Helfand was there to represent the City of Bellaire. The whole thing took only about forty-five minutes, and after a few weeks, we had our decision.

"The Fifth Circuit denied our appeal," my mom told me. I just stared at her, speechless. "It's okay, don't worry. Everything is going to be okay."

The judgment said the court was upholding Judge Harmon's decision based on qualified immunity because it was felt that we hadn't "shown a genuine dispute of material fact."

But Siegel wasn't a quitter, and within days of the judgment, he filed a second petition before the full court of all seventeen judges on the Fifth Circuit. We were rejected again, although three judges did come back and write legal briefs on our behalf. But it didn't look good.

"So what's our next step?" I asked Siegel.

"The next step," Siegel said, "is the United States Supreme Court."

Siegel didn't seem particularly phased by the idea that we'd bring this case before the high court, but it blew my mind. Each year, the Supreme Court receives tens of thousands of petitions, and it only elects to hear about one hundred. But that wasn't the only hurdle for us. In order to pay for our case going to the United States Supreme Court, my parents had to sell their Bellaire home.

I said before that I wanted my parents to sell that home because of all the bad memories the Woodstock home held, but I didn't want them to have to sell the house like this.

As for Siegel, he had basically worked on our case for a year without ever mentioning money. He knew that we were underwater from our medical bills, but he never seemed worried about getting paid. But soon the time came to pay for expenses.

"Don't worry about it, Robbie," my mom told me. "You're worth it."

Yeah, that was easy for her to say, but feelings of guilt came rushing back to me.

For several weeks, we waited to hear whether our petition would be chosen. We followed multiple Supreme Court blogs for clues. Finally, we got the news. The Supreme Court, against all odds, had chosen our case. Siegel was ecstatic, and so were we. The most powerful court in the world would hear little ole Robbie Tolan's case!

The justices reached out to the City of Bellaire to see if they prepared a response to our petition, but of course, not only had the City of Bellaire not prepared a response, they had no plan to do so. That's when the high court ordered them to respond to the petition.

We watched as the Supreme Court asked the lower courts for every deposition, every piece of evidence—anything that was associated with the case. The justices met to discuss our case an unprecedented eleven times.

The Supreme Court was truly our court of last chance, and if we lost, we were officially dead. If we won, then the case would be sent back to the Fifth Circuit, which would hear our case again, or they could boot it back to the district court room of Judge Harmon, which was not our hope at all. But first, we needed to see if we could win.

I prayed like I'd never prayed before. I remember being in the hospital and asking God to spare my life, and I prayed with the same vigor as then. I asked Pastor Caldwell, who had a church with over fifteen thousand members, to pray for us. In fact, members of the church were encouraged to each pick a Supreme Court judge and pray for that judge exclusively. The prayer's intention was that they would rule with a clean and unbiased heart.

The verdict came when I was half asleep. The phone rang on May 5, 2014, and it was my mom.

"We won!" she said, half shouting, half screaming.

"Huh?" I said, still fumbling with the phone. "What are you talking about?"

"We won in the Supreme Court! We won, Robbie!"

I suddenly got ramrod straight on the bed, sorta like I used to get at Aunt Carolyn's right after I was released from the hospital.

"Are you serious?" I asked, still not believing that what my mother was saying was real. We'd lost so many times, at the criminal trial, the civil trial, and the appeals, and there didn't seem to be a light at the end of the tunnel. But dammit, that light wasn't another train designed to crash into us, but a true light of hope that we just might win.

"The Supreme Court ruled unanimously in our favor," my mom told me. "And two of the most conservative justices, Alito and Scalia, even wrote opinions in our favor."

This was huge. For the first time in nearly two decades, the United States Supreme Court ruled unanimously on a civil rights case, and this one was precedent setting. It basically said that you can't just take the police's word about what happened during a confrontation with the police. If the law already puts its thumb on the scales of justice by giving police officers qualified immunity, then you can't say that my point of view as the victim isn't relevant, or that the jury shouldn't see it. And even the most pro–law enforcement Supreme Court justices on the court agreed in *Tolan v. Cotton.*

Justice Alito said:

[T]he granting of review in this case sets a precedent that, if followed in other cases, will very substantially alter the Court's practice.... In my experience, a substantial percentage of the civil appeals heard each year by the courts of appeals present the question whether the evidence in the summary judgment record is just enough or not quite enough to support a grant of summary judgment. The present case falls into that very large category.

There is no confusion in the courts of appeals about the standard to be applied in ruling on a summary judgment motion, and the Court of Appeals invoked the correct standard here. Thus, the only issue is whether the relevant evidence, viewed in the light most favorable to the nonmoving party, is sufficient to support a judgment for that party. In the courts of appeals, cases presenting this question are utterly routine. There is no question that this case is important for the parties, but the same is true for a great many other cases that fall into the same category.

Basically, the Supreme Court ruled that the lower courts "fail[ed] to credit evidence that contradicted some of its key factual conclusions." In other words, the lower courts only gave credence to the evidence that favored Cotton and didn't give the same importance to evidence that favored us. And since qualified immunity gave a wide latitude to government employees who harmed citizens, courts could put their finger on the scale by trying to figure out what the officer was thinking or feeling. So according to the Supreme Court, Melinda Harmon had granted summary judgment based on qualified immunity to a police officer in a civil rights case, and the Fifth circuit had wrongly upheld her decision.

"[The Fifth U.S. Circuit Court of Appeals] should have acknowledged and credited Tolan's evidence with regard to the lighting, his mother's demeanor, whether he shouted words that were an overt threat, and his positioning during the shooting," the Supreme Court ruling stated.

High-powered lawyers like Eric Del Pozo of the Chicago

mega-firm Jenner & Block had filed an amicus brief on behalf of the NAACP Legal Defense Fund, and he thought it was precedent setting.

"It rights the ship a little bit," Del Pozo told *The Atlantic* magazine. "[Courts don't want] to foster a perception that the courthouse doors are closed to persons with meritorious claims."

It was the first time in a decade that the court had ruled against a police officer, and over five hundred different court cases have used my ruling in their own cases against the police. Of course, the City of Bellaire did not agree with the ruling.

"The plaintiffs have alleged their personal beliefs that race was a factor in the adverse actions taken against them by the defendants in this case, but such a personal belief, unsubstantiated, cannot support their claim of denial of equal protection of the laws," Helfand said in response.

But then Helfand said something that blew me away because it showed just how out of touch he and, by proxy, the City of Bellaire were. To counteract the idea that Edwards and Cotton had racially profiled me, he dropped this jewel.

"You can't tell just by looking at him what his race is," Helfand told the *Houston Chronicle,* speaking about me. "Long before this incident, I thought Bobby Tolan was a great baseball player for the Cincinnati Reds. I always thought Bobby Tolan was Hispanic."

Oh, so that's it. Edwards and Cotton thought that I was Hispanic, and not black, so they couldn't possibly be racially profiling me. I'll go ask Jose Cruz, Jr. about what he has to say about that.

Mark Anthony Neal, an African American professor at Duke University, said it best when talking about race and policing.

"The law wants to deny the racial reality of these cases," Neal told *USA Today*. "It wants to suppress the racial dynamics of violence against black bodies because once race is on the table, it changes how everybody reads these cases. What the Supreme Court essentially has said—without saying it very blatantly—is that well no you can't suppress race in this case."

That statement spoke directly to how the City of Bellaire looked at my case from the start and how their lawyer, Bill Helfand, defended them. Forget about being colorblind, the City of Bellaire, and the courts, had been color deniers.

Law professors from throughout the country also weighed in on our case since it was so precedent setting. Most thought that we'd still have an uphill battle, but we were still in the fight.

"Tolan may ultimately lose the case; however, this is still a victory [for Tolan] because the summary judgments by the lower courts represented such one-sided deference to the police claims," Rogers Smith, a political science professor at the University of Pennsylvania, told *USA Today*. "It was clear the police had made a mistake in thinking the car was stolen and the police ended up shooting an innocent young man."

I can't emphasize how important this Supreme Court verdict was to me, not just as a legal ruling, but as a personal sense of validation. From the time of my shooting to when the justices ruled in my favor, I felt like a man without a country. Yes, the justice system was there for me to use, like any citizen, but I felt like I was an invisible man to them—a black man whose human rights were subservient to the rights of the police, even though I'd done nothing to cause my shooting.

The fact that conservatives and liberals on the court had

come together reminded me that I was indeed an American, an American whose theoretical rights were just as real as anyone else's rights. Yes, I knew that my case didn't end with their ruling, but I take pride in knowing that this one ruling has been cited in over five hundred other cases. My shooting had meaning, much more than my own trials and tribulations, but to people I'd never meet. In a way, I was the counterpoint to Dred Scott being told that he had no rights that a white man was bound to respect. I had to be respected, and my life had to be respected. And that lifted my spirit.

However, one shouldn't think that the criminal justice system has succeeded. The victory, even at 9-0, was an illusive one. The Supreme Court vacated the decision of the Fifth Circuit and ordered the lower courts to consider all evidence, not just the evidence favoring Cotton. Unfortunately, the case was sent back to Judge Harmon, who had initially thrown it out.

Great.

Before I continue about my case, let me talk about the strength of my mom. I put a lot of work into my case, but she has been the stalwart, the point man for us, and despite the odds, she never lost sight of her goal. She wanted justice when I was in the hospital room, and nearly ten years later, she still wanted justice. If she fell into any type of depression or funk, she never let me see it.

Our time with Martin Siegel was done, and we couldn't have been happier with his work. But he was exclusively an appellate attorney, which meant that we needed to find another attorney who could represent us in Judge Harmon's courtroom, and that lawyer was Benjamin Crump. I'm not sure how we got hooked up with Crump, but I think it was because my mom bugged the hell out of his officer to represent us.

Crump first made his national mark when he represented Trayvon Martin's family during the George Zimmerman trial in 2012. Based in Florida, he worked on civil rights cases with his law partner Darryl Parks, as Parks & Crump. Also assisting was attorney Darryl Washington, whose law offices were located in Dallas. One of the things that impressed us about Crump is that we had a candid conversation at my parent's house in Houston, and he talked about how he could have built his law career around any type of law, but civil rights was in his DNA. He felt compelled to fight for civil rights and justice.

I think that was the difference in our lawyers. Lawyers like Greenwood, Morris, and Siegel really demonstrated that they were on our side and the side of justice. It's not that the Bergs didn't want the same thing, but in a show don't tell world, the aforementioned lawyers definitely showed, while the Bergs were busy laughing with our opponents. Guess who we liked more?

I also loved how Crump handled the press. He was out there advocating for us.

"All this family wants is their day in court," Crump said. "We have to send a message to police when they act in this outrageous conduct. The law has to protect citizens whether they are black, white, or Hispanic."

But Crump had bad news for us. Judge Harmon hadn't been impressed by the Supreme Court's ruling and basically said that she didn't care. The day before the trial was supposed to begin, she was even considering dismissing the case.

"I'm very tempted to grant it [dismissal] but I'm not going to right now....I think the Supreme Court sent it back to the circuit so they could reanalyze my case. The 5th Circuit didn't want to do that, so they punted to me. And I don't think...they would ever be satisfied if we didn't take this case to trial....I have a lot of faith in my opinion....I thought it was right the first time."

"We've got to try to get Judge Harmon off this case," Crump told us. "If not, we're going to need to think about settling this case."

I couldn't believe that the criminal justice system could allow a district court judge to pretty much ignore a precedent, simply because she thought she was right the first time. No, Judge Harmon, nine justices told you that you weren't. I don't know if it was ego, or hurt feelings, or what, but she was a stumbling block that needed to be removed. I didn't spend eight years in the courts to simply allow her to block us.

So Crump filed an emergency motion for recusal, arguing that Judge Harmon had made comments saying that she was confident in her original decision, despite the Supreme Court's ruling.

At first, we didn't hear anything from Judge Harmon on that matter, but she did make it a point to release an eighteen-page opinion that barred us from introducing Major League Baseball players like my cousin Ken Griffey Jr. from testifying as expert witnesses in my case, something that a federal magistrate judge had allowed us to do. We wanted them to speak as experts on how the bullet in my gut had harmed my potential earnings as a baseball player, but Judge Harmon ruled that they needed to provide "reports" as experts, and since they hadn't, they were out.

It was furious because it seemed like this judge had it out for us. And then came her ruling about recusing herself from the case. She denied our request, saying that she had "never expressed a personal bias or prejudice against Robert R. Tolan or in favor of Jeffrey Cotton."

Give me a break. The only thing Judge Harmon hadn't done in favor of Cotton was to pin badges on his chest. And again, with an arrogance that I didn't understand, she reiterated, "I have a lot of faith in my opinion," despite being vacated by the Supreme Court. It was clear to me that when Judge Harmon wrote that she hadn't displayed a "deep-seated favoritism or antagonism that would make fair judgment impossible," she wanted to make sure that she stayed on this case and that her finger was still on those scales for Cotton. That's the only way I could see it.

But Crump didn't quit. He noted that Judge Harmon had based her decision to stay on the case by only pointing to one of two federal statutes, but she hadn't responded to a statute stating that a federal judge "shall disqualify himself in any proceeding in which his impartiality might reasonably be questioned."

Judge Harmon denied our initial request by stating, "When a judge makes a ruling or says or does something in the course of pretrial or trial proceedings, impartiality cannot reasonably be questioned simply because one side wins and the other loses."

It was a hopeless battle, and to be honest, we were getting weary. The prospect of going to trial in Judge Harmon's courtroom, and almost certainly coming out with nothing, seemed like a forgone conclusion. If she still believed in her original opinion, then, as Crump told us, she sure as hell still believed in the conclusion she drew the first time. It was time to settle, I realized.

But I was going to have to convince my mom, who didn't want to give up the fight.

"We are not going to let them get away with this," my mom argued.

"But we're not. I'm just tired," I told her. "We've been at this for eight years. Eight long years of my life, and at some point, it's time for me to move on with my life. I can't let this one bullet consume me forever."

I was tired of this shit. I had just turned thirty. Nearly 75 percent of my twenties had been fighting this battle. I had spent all of my twenties dealing with this shit, and no, I didn't have a nervous breakdown. I could have been a normal person who does things like have fun or go to the club and talk to pretty women. But instead, I've gotta worry about how I'm seen in the media. This incident was always hanging over my life. I needed to move on to something else.

My mom wasn't trying to hear any of that. If there was one true cost of this long fight, particularly when it came to settling the case, it was the relationship between me and my mom. Settling caused a deep rift between me and the woman who'd talked to me when I was still in the womb, who'd nurtured me to the point of surviving when my twin hadn't, and who'd fought for me at every turn. She couldn't understand that my life was my life and not a cause célèbre.

"We were treated like shit, and I wanted white folks to understand that this is happening to American citizens, and everybody should be upset when an American citizen isn't treated right," Marian recounted. "I just felt like since Bobby was a former baseball player, that they might listen for the first time, and that we might use what we could to make change for the greater good. And I didn't care about what it would cost. And I didn't care about selling my house. And I wanted to win because I knew God saved Robbie for a reason. And whatever he wanted us to do, we were going to do it at all costs. And I win."

"I don't think Robbie and I were in conflict until the case went back to [Judge Harmon], and I think he had a nervous break-down. I was ready to fight, I was ready to go back to the Supreme Court."

What my mom didn't realize is that, if we kept fighting, we would be fighting for another five or so years. I would be in my mid-thirties still dealing with this. I couldn't take it, and we argued, hard, because I think she thought I was giving up. But I wasn't giving up; I was giving in to having a life without this bur-den on my shoulders each and every day.

It was emotional between me and my mom. We were beef-ing hard, and it was difficult to deal with because the one person who'd been my biggest advocate was now my biggest adversary when it came to stopping this whole thing. She just wasn't hav-ing it.

The point at which she began to see this case, and the rest of my life, through my eyes was when Ben Crump told me that the judge had thrown not only the baseball witnesses off the case, but also the City of Bellaire, my mom and dad, and Anthony. So going forward, it would only be me versus Cotton in a civil suit. So here we were, me with no money versus a cop with no money.

"Now I just represent you," Crump told me. "If you want to settle, that's what we'll do."

Crump told us that we were actually in a weaker position due to the fact that Judge Harmon was going to be on the bench, so we needed to settle now before the City of Bellaire decided to wait us out.

I told my mom that, at least when it came to the legal aspect, my case was over. "We did what we could," I said. "We fought."

My mom was livid.

"I don't want to hear that shit!" my mom said angrily. "I told you that I'm not settling, and I don't care if you're tired, I'm not tired!"

I was so conflicted because I didn't want to make a deal if the person who had been fighting for me didn't want it. It physically broke me. I passed out to the point of not being able to walk.

I was angry because my dad had had a full life. My mom had had a full life. And what about me? What am I gonna do, fight this for the rest of my life? I've had no life.

I called my mom crying and barely able to talk. I wanted to settle and get out from under this. Finally, my mom told me to take the deal.

"I'm sorry," I sobbed to my mom. "I'm sorry."

"Don't worry, Robbie, take the deal," she said.

It was the hardest day of my life.

"I knew that Robbie couldn't take it," said Marian. "He was in conflict because he didn't want to go against me, and I wanted to keep fighting. I wanted to keep fighting for those people who can't fight for themselves, but I couldn't keep fighting and risk losing him. I knew I would have to fight in a different way."

After a bit of negotiation, the City of Bellaire agreed to settle the case for $110,000. It was a pittance compared to the medical and legal fees, totaling almost a million dollars, that were drowning me, and I don't look at the settlement as a victory. It was simply a conclusion to a long personal nightmare.

After the settlement, we left the courtroom to face a gaggle of reporters, who all wanted to know what was next.

"Nobody can call him a thug," Crump told reporters. "No police union can try to defame his name or character. He has no criminal history. He comes from a good family."

"I'm satisfied that I get to move on and tell my story," I told reporters as I left court. "We need to continue to work to effect change. Until that happens, it's going to keep happening. Young black men, unarmed, are going to keep getting shot until we do something about it."

"Though I still have my son, I've had to watch his dreams and a part of his spirit die," my mom told reporters. "We've given up so much as a family to get a chance at justice. A chance at peace. A chance at being whole again."

# CHAPTER 10

# A LIFE WITHOUT TRUE JUSTICE

**Rumain Brisbon, 34, Phoenix, Arizona—December 2, 2014**

Rumain Brisbon, a thirty-four-year-old African American father of four, was shot and killed in Phoenix, Arizona, by Officer Mark Rine. An anonymous tip indicated that Brisbon was involved in a drug deal, and when Officer Rine approached Brisbon, he claimed to see Brisbon put something in his waistband. After Officer Rine confronted him, Brisbon ran and was soon chased by Officer Rine to Brisbon's girlfriend's apartment, where according to the police, there was a struggle. Officer Rine claimed to fear for his life, thinking that Brisbon had a gun, so he shot Brisbon twice, killing him. Later it was found that Brisbon was unarmed, with only a bottle of oxycodone in his pocket. Officer Rine was not charged in the shooting.

So where does this leave us? Where does it leave my family? Where does it leave other black victims of police racial profiling and police violence? Where does it leave the City of Bellaire, the Bellaire Police Department, and the black citizens who are doing ordinary things in this country, but who can be profiled to the point of being shot? Where does it leave the criminal justice system, which maintains that black people can be shot as long as a judge considers it reasonable? And lastly, where does it leave me?

For my family, December 31, 2008, was a devastating day. They watched as their only child was shot and nearly killed. They sat in the hospital, praying prayers as they'd never done before, hoping that the bullet that resided in my liver didn't do any more damage. They saw the stress nearly kill my dad to the point where he required a double heart bypass. They took me in when I couldn't go back to the house in which I'd grown up. They filled rows of the courthouse and went through the emotional roller coaster of watching a jury of their peers essentially say that their family member deserved that bullet because they felt Sgt. Cotton was being "reasonable."

Bullshit.

What's not reasonable is the damage to my parents and to our relationship that one bullet caused, something I can't over-emphasize. You know how people like to say that the victims of shootings aren't the only victims, well, I know that firsthand now. Even though they hadn't been the target of the bullet that entered my chest, my family was just as wounded as me when it came to this ordeal.

My parents lost their home in order to pay the legal fees for my appeal. I watched as my elderly father, who should have been living a relaxed life, had to start driving for Uber in order to make ends meet. Watching this, I couldn't help but think about the Rudyard Kipling poem, "If," where he writes, "If you can force your heart and nerve and sinew, to serve your turn long after they are gone. And so hold on when there is nothing in you, except the Will which says to them: 'Hold on.'" My father embodied the hero who did his best to hold on as his son struggled to find jus-tice, with no guarantee that he'd find it.

But my greatest regret centers around how this shooting caused a fissure between me and my mom. I watched my mom, that relentless warrior for justice, grow frustrated with the sys-tem, and sometimes me, as the reality hit that we wouldn't get Cotton and Edwards to apologize for their actions. For years, my mom and I fought and argued about how far to take this struggle, and whether quitting was preferable to living a life that seemed suspended in uncertainty. My mom looked at the big picture, the one that said holding the police responsible for what they did to me was as important for my own life as it was for the lives of countless black people who'd find themselves in the same unjust situation. And the Supreme Court decision was a justification for her point of view. Robbie Tolan had moved from being a local story about another police shooting to a case study that would be cited by courts for years to come.

But what about my life? What about a life that I wanted? My mom couldn't understand that I didn't want to live my life as one long court case, as one long symbol of police brutality. In some ways, the extraordinary circumstances that I was thrust into made me yearn for the ordinary life of the anonymous person on the street. I craved it, that sense that I could move on from this bullet in my chest and into a new Robbie Tolan. A Robbie who laughed again, who loved again, who had dreams again.

I have no doubt that my mom wanted the same thing from me, but when two people are competing to define someone's future, I think it's easy to become myopic, and that's what happened with my mom. So our relationship suffered as I didn't want to disappoint her, and she wanted to fight for me.

And it would be nice to say that everything is okay with us, but it's not completely. I think as long as we live, my mom, ever the fighter, will think that I should have fought to the end instead of taking the settlement. But I knew better, even when I would literally break down in tears, overwhelmed by the idea that I was disappointing my mother.

But I learned that no matter how we both thought we were doing what was right, I had to take control of my life. To get my story out to the world. To control my own destiny. And that meant that my mom and I would have to heal both together and separately. No one, not even my mom, who I love to the moon and beyond, was responsible for what I was to become and how I would define myself. I wasn't going to have my life defined by the injustice of a bullet, and that meant that even if my mom thought otherwise, I was going to have to move on with my life. However, here's what I know. We'll get through this.

We wouldn't get a settlement that sent a message to the world that you can't just shoot black people when you want and get away with it.

What about black victims of police racial profiling and police violence? Not just the high-profile victims who are shot, killed, and then turned into social media hashtags, but also the ordinary black people who walk around living ordinary lives? Do they feel more reassured that the police will be held accountable when, at best, a mistake is made or, at worst, a police officer purposefully harms them? I don't think so. I think because of my little case, black people around this country are that much less secure.

Black lives matter for real, and it's not just a slogan. If we're going to be a country where every citizen is asked to believe in the police, then we're going to need to trust the police, and I don't think any black person, at least any sane black person, should blindly trust the police. This isn't to say that you hate the police or, hell, that you love the police. Hating or loving the police isn't germane to whether or not black people can expect to live on this earth without being harassed or killed by the people who are supposed to be protecting and serving their citizens.

If I come off as sad and bitter, then so be it. All I can do is react to the world that I see. I see Charlottesville, where a young woman, Heather Heyer, gets killed by a neo-Nazi, and Donald Trump, who currently occupies the White House, openly coddles the neo-Nazis as having "good people on both sides." We live in a world where the leader of the free world instructs police to not to worry about "being rough" with potential suspects. How in the world am I to believe that I live in an America where my rights are protected and the bullet that entered my chest is justified by a man who sees me as a nothing?

I don't.

I see an increasingly cruel America, an America where Colin Kaepernick and NFL players kneel over the issue of police brutality, and white America gets fake mad about "disrespecting the flag." How can I believe that police departments from Los Angeles to New York City are going to take the shootings of black people seriously, when white people want to turn an intentional blind eye to the issue?

As a black person, it makes you want to scream, because no matter what we do, we're told to keep quiet. We march in the streets, and we're told that we shouldn't march. We silently protest, we're told that we shouldn't protest. But when we're shot the silence about our lives is deafening.

Where does it leave the City of Bellaire and the Bellaire Police Department? In a city that has historically turned a blind eye to the idea that their police have racially profiled black people, there was finally some movement. The NAACP and the city came up with a plan to allow citizens to contact it about racial profiling, and that is a positive. But what does it say about the morals of the City of Bellaire officials when they'd rather pay their lawyers over $450,000 in legal fees instead of paying us a reasonable settlement. That's four times as much money as we received in the settlement. In the end, the City of Bellaire filled the pockets of lawyers and left us with medical and legal debt. How inhumane is that? I honestly don't know how they can live with themselves, but it gives me a clear understanding that I can never live in a city where my life is worth so little.

There's a reason why police department unions backed someone like Donald Trump, and it didn't have a damn thing to do with jobs or draining the swamp. The election of Barack Obama as president was seen as a threat to the white supremacist system in this country, and so for every reaction, you have an opposite reaction. And if Obama represented a "Yes We Can" ethos, then Trump was the "No You Won't" response. And for black people who were out there in the streets saying that Black Lives Matter after every police shooting, the blowback was millions of Americans telling the police departments that our lives didn't matter, and here's the guy to reiterate that as a fact.

Will the City of Bellaire change its police department so that another black person won't be shot for driving their own car, parking in front of their own house, and rising to defend their mother? I doubt it. Because where is the incentive? It's not coming from the top of the country, so it sure as hell isn't trickling down to the local police departments of this country.

Again, if you think I'm bitter about that, you're damn right I am. It means that even though I've gone though a decade-long struggle to be seen as an American citizen, as a human being worthy of respect and justice, I can still be shot today by the police and be right back in the same situation, unanimous Supreme Court decisions notwithstanding. No citizen of this great country should have to have that as a daily reality, and yet black people do, validated by a president of the United States who thinks police brutality is a punch line to a joke. My chest wound, something I'll live with for the rest of my life, is a counterpoint to his assertion, and it's not funny at all.

When it comes to the criminal justice system, we're always talking about how we've been raised to believe in truth, justice, and the American way and about the blind justice to which each American is entitled. And yet we have laws that say that if a police officer, because he has a tough job, shoots you, and people think it's reasonable even if mistaken, then it's all good. How can I believe that the criminal justice system works for me as a black man when the evidence in front of me says that it doesn't? What I see is a criminal justice system designed to keep me down. To keep me in a cage. To keep me looking over my shoulder for situations out of my control. I no longer believe that a jury of my peers can empathize with who I am, unless you start having juries filled with people of color: Blacks, Latinos, Asians, and others who see their community members as human beings and not racial stereotypes. Nor do we need juries who look at the police as being beyond reproach.

Finally, where does it leave me? I've been the focus of this decade-long drama, the person who stood up for his mother and took a bullet for it. I'm the one who went into surgery and had his life turned upside down and broken, to the point where I had to not only re-evaluate my dreams, but also decide whether or not

I wanted to live another day so that I could create new dreams. I was the one who desperately wanted to hide from the world, who found solace in my Unknown 90 anonymity, but in the end, I looked the world in the eye and kept it moving.

In the end, I'm proud of myself. I didn't let a bullet stop me. I fought for everything that came my way and kept my integrity as I did it. I fought so that I could retain my sanity, even when the days got dark. I fought to do what was right for my family and to protect them whenever I could. I fought my lawyers and the legal system, to the point where the United States Supreme Court would unanimously rule in my favor. And I learned something about myself.

I was going to be okay. At some point, I realized that I was stronger than I thought I was—that I could look death in the eye and not only live, but thrive. I'll never say that I am better off because I was shot, because no one improves by having their body violated. So that's not it. I learned about an inner strength that I had but hadn't tapped. Maybe it was always there, generated from my mother's prayers when I was in her womb trying to survive when my twin didn't. I don't know where strength came from, and I could spend years trying to figure it out. But despite the fact that I'm in so much medical and legal debt that I can't see the end of the it, I'm not scared.

And that's my broader message for black people and those of us who support the Black Lives Matter movement. We have to not be scared. We have to demand that the criminal justice system, including everyone from the police officer in the patrol car to those who get selected for jury duty, be equal and fair to all. Black people don't hate cops; hell, even after everything I've been through, I still don't hate cops. However, I think I can say that black folks do hate oppression. And the line between a good cop and a bad cop isn't simply when one decides to double check a license plate. A cop should know that the city that pays him is more interested in justice than "Just Us." And if you spend three times as much money on legal fees in order to not pay your own resident for wrongdoing, then you're creating a system of immoral justice.

My fight against Jeffrey Cotton and John Edwards wasn't personal. I'm sure they could be wonderful people who love their family and kids and do all of the nice things that nice people do. They could also be bad people who kick kittens, trip old people, and curse out mothers on Mother's Day. Who knows? But I do know that none of that matters. What I wanted from them was accountability, and yet since my shooting, Sgt. Cotton has been promoted to lieutenant.

Are you fucking kidding me? While on paid administrative leave, he was basically on a year-and-a-half-long vacation. I am fucking broke, up to my eyeballs in debt, and I lost my career. And I got nothing. Nothing. Not even an apology.

Also, where is the sense of remorse that doesn't come from me interpreting their actions, but comes from their own words? I wanted Cotton and Edwards, and the City of Bellaire for that matter, to say two words:

"I'm sorry."

I can't tell you how cathartic it would have been to hear those words, and not just for me and my family, but also for the two officers. But even the legalese in the settlement had the weasel words that avoided any sign that anyone involved in my shooting regretted it. The agreement stated that the city and Cotton "have consistently denied liability in this matter" but that the municipality is paying the money "in compromise and settlement of a disputed claim to avoid further expense of litigation and disruption of public service."

Basically, they just wanted us to go away. Or as our attorney Darryl Washington once said at the conclusion of our case, "This guy was not punished, but he was rewarded after he shot Robbie [being promoted to lieutenant]. Even if they say it was a mistake, you apologize for mistakes. This is something the city has failed to do, refused to do."

Asking for and receiving forgiveness is a human need; it allows us to look forward without feeling that we have the burden of our past hanging over us. I have the power to forgive these two officers, and I do. Not because I'm a bigger man or because I want to absolve them. My forgiveness does none of that for them. I forgive them for me. It completes my humanity. By not offering up their remorse, they are now saddled with the unconscious understanding that they did wrong and never said they were sorry. But that's now between them and their God.

I'm good.

But I will say this. Just because I'm good, it doesn't mean that America itself doesn't need a culture change. Racism and injustice have a way of acting as a cancer, and it metastasizes into our society in other areas. The callousness we feel when we turn off our brains when black person after black person is killed by the police is the same mechanism of empathy we turn off when a mass murderer uses a semi-automatic weapon to shoot and kill over fifty people in Las Vegas, and no one remembers it as being extraordinary after a month goes by. Just another day in America where gun violence is normalized, and of course, it's never the right time to talk about gun control.

This means that for the All Lives Matter crew, the ones who don't think police brutality exists, you'd better start recognizing that if you don't recognize that black deaths at the hands of the police is a symptom of the larger epidemic of gun violence, you're going to see white bodies violated by bullets more and more. As Malcolm X once said, the chickens tend to come home to roost if you allow violence in one area, it'll come back to bite you in your own area.

Despite all of this, deep within the recesses of my being, I still hold out hope that America can be better. That we can change this toxic culture that sees some people as human beings and others as nothing. Why do I believe this? Because of the wonderful people I met throughout this journey.

I met good people: from the doctors and nurses in the hospital, who were as important to my recovery as the surgery and the medicine pumping through my veins, to the Harris County DA's Office, with Clint Greenwood and Steve Morris championing my cause. I'm forever grateful for their generosity and selflessness in helping me achieve justice.

An interview with the filmmaker Keith Beauchamp led to me meeting some amazing people in social justice. Beauchamp produces and hosts an Investigation Discovery channel program called *The Injustice Files*, and he was interested in featuring me and my story in a segment called, "Hood of Suspicion."

An annual show, each year, it has a theme that tackles social justice and civil rights. For example, the previous show had dealt with modern-day lynchings. In our episode, Keith was tackling racial profiling and the "stand your ground" law that had been much discussed in connection with the George Zimmerman killing of Trayvon Martin.

At first, I was reluctant to appear on the show, but I saw that Beauchamp had a long history of chronicling injustice. His first documentary, at twenty-three years old, was *The Untold Story of Emmett Louis Till*, a film that took him nine years to make and eventually led to the cold case being opened. And since Beauchamp had experienced racial profiling himself in Baton Rouge, he understood what I was going through.

Beauchamp flew out with his producer and spent two days with me before we started shooting. He spent the entire day hanging with my family, taking us to dinner, and sharing stories of his childhood. By the time the cameras started rolling, it was more like we were old friends than filmmaker and subject. The cool part is that this piece wasn't just about me. It was about a number of other cases, particularly in Homer, Louisiana, where he did a story about their infamous police department.

Later, Investigation Discovery invited us to attend the Television Critics Association conference in Los Angeles, a huge convention where all of television gathers to present and promote their new shows for the upcoming season. I sat on a panel with Investigation Discovery's senior vice president, Sara "Koz" Kozak, Beauchamp, and Carolyn McKinstry, a survivor of the infamous Sixteenth Street Baptist Church bombing in Birmingham, Alabama, in 1963, when the Ku Klux Klan murdered four little black girls. I'd done my research on the panel, and I appreciated the opportunity to tell my story.

During the discussion, I reveled in every utterance of Carolyn McKinstry, who with her soft soothing tone and her mild-mannered demeanor, spoke of survivor's guilt, which up to that point I'd thought was imaginary. I'd never really had a conversation with someone who had gone through something similar to my experience. I'd only spoken with people with doctorates, folks who loved telling me that I needed to be strong and brave and that it was okay to be upset and confused, but none of them had personally gone through my trauma. It was all theory to them, stuff they'd learned in school. But Ms. McKinstry was the first person to convince me that I wasn't alone.

Everything she said I had thought about or experienced. And hearing her gave me great comfort. After the panel, I told her how much I appreciated her story and that it was an honor to meet with her. But it wasn't the last time we'd be together.

A few weeks later, at the Paley Center in New York, I joined McKinstry; Beauchamp; Kerry Kennedy, the daughter of Robert F. Kennedy and founder of the Robert F. Kennedy Center for Justice and Human Rights; First Amendment crusader, former RFK aide, and civil rights luminary John Seigenthaler; and world-renowned journalist and anchor and our master of ceremonies Harry Smith.

After the panel, we all went to dinner, where I was honored to hear John Seigenthaler say to me, "I was very impressed with you. You're young, well spoken, good looking." At this, he gave me a light-hearted punch to the chest. "And I'll tell you what Robbie, you're the face of racial profiling."

And that was when I knew that I was put on this earth for more than simply being a victim. I was thrust into this role, and

I wasn't prepared for it, but from that day forward, I wasn't going to hide. I wasn't going to be Unknown 90 anymore, and I was going to be that face of racial profiling, of police violence. The fact that I had lived and others had died was not going to stop me.

But I don't want you to think that good people, or being a good person, is enough. If you're a good person who doesn't help change society in a meaningful way, then you're complicit in how that society treats me as a black man. I need you out there in the street protesting, in the ballot box voting, and on the police civilian review boards holding law enforcement accountable. Because that's the only time that I will know that you actually care about who I am, and others like me.

Because to not know that is to find yourself struggling to exist. After dozens of heartbreaks over the years, I'd fallen into a deep depression to the point where I considered taking my own life. It took prayer, lots of prayer, to help God break me out of that funk. It wasn't gradual; it didn't happen over time, but all of the sudden.

I had spent so much time away from God, trying to climb the wrong ladder as I tried to mend my physical and mental selves, I know that He had to work hard to bring me back to square one. He knew that in order for me to have a chance of becoming the man He intended me to be, He needed to give me the strength to wipe the slate clean, and we would be able to start over together. I had to go through an emotional and spiritual bankruptcy to do that.

I literally woke up one day and the depression was gone. Like all things with God, there was something unexplainable in the air. I walked outside and the sun shined brighter, and the wind blew differently. It was peaceful again, and I felt alive, like I had died and been reborn. The worst was behind me, and it was time for the restoration.

After God broke the stronghold that depression had on my life, I felt daily changes in my spirit. God got me through this ordeal, and now it was time to pay Him back. Every day, God continues to reconstruct my spirit, and as such, I know I am on the righteous path. And now I know that the incident on December 31, 2008, was not the ending, but the beginning. I fully believe that I was ordained with a divine purpose at birth, and I have to make sure that I follow that purpose for the rest of my life.

I don't know what God has in store for my life, but I doubt that most people do. But I do know that I want to help people, lots and lots of people. I've always been able to recognize the needs of people, going back to when I was young and my mom took me to help out at homeless shelters. I've had countless blessings that have inspired me to bless and inspire others, even if I lack means. The bullet I took to my chest inadvertently created a stronger human being than what was there before. I know who I am, and I know that I'm a powerful vessel for making change in this country, and I believe that God is going to use me in that capacity.

I can't wait.

# ACKNOWLEDGMENTS

This is the part of the book I've been dreading the most, simply because when it's time to say thank you to all the people who've been in your corner, you're almost guaranteed to leave someone out. Who do I acknowledge? Do I include everyone I can think of? Or just my immediate family so that I don't have to worry about leaving anyone out? Do I mention one group of friends but not another? Do I thank the people I interact with every day? My best friends know how I feel about them; do I really need to thank them? See what I mean? That's why I put this off until the last possible second. It's already hard enough to do this without tearing up. So if I somehow do forget to mention you, I beg for your forgiveness...or, it probably just wasn't meant to be, lol.

I THANK GOD for sparing my life for a greater purpose and continuing to order my steps. I am thankful for His grace and mercy.

Mom and Dad, I cannot thank you enough for your unconditional love and unceasing (and sometimes undeserved) support. I was a weird little kid, but you always encouraged my eccentricities and never hampered my creativity. One day I hope to have children who feel as much love and encouragement as I felt from the both of you. I love you both so much. I hope I make you proud.

This part of the Acknowledgments was the toughest to write, as I feared the possibility of not capturing my extreme gratitude to my village and my support system. To my aunts Carolyn and Tammy and my uncle Charles, I'm trying not to curse in my thank yous, so for fear of being uncouth, I'll just say that you all are beyond amazing. I thank you for always stepping up. From Odyssey of the Mind competitions out of town, to Little League games, to press conferences and sitting front and center in court, you all were ALWAYS there. Thank you Ken and Melissa for every bit of support and everything else you've done for my family and me over the years, and for agreeing to do the foreword for this book. Y'all know I don't like asking for anything, but you said yes without hesitation and I'm forever grateful. My sister, Cathy Carroll!! I thank God for you and that "Chica-go-getter" attitude!!! Had you not "harassed" the Winans brothers in Houston, this book would have never happened the way it did. I wish I could afford to hire you as my personal hype man. I wish I could tell little stories about each of the following people that expresses my gratitude, but I'm rushing to get this in, so thanks to: Chad and Toni, Kacy, Aunt Mel, Aunt Theresa, Tony Scott, Chasen, Anthony, Uncle Mike, Gale, EZ, Kevin Jackson and the Jackson 5, Lewis and Bridgette, Jerry and Rachel, Courtney and Adrienne, Randy, Pam Cox, Bryan-Michael Cox, Jim and Beverly, Carlos and Audrey, Treani, Aunt Evelyn and crew, Griffey family, Littleton and Harding families, Lisa, JD Elliby, and the rest of them Trahans. Man, I feel like I'm forgetting someone; please don't beat me up when you see me. But thank you all for investing in me. You all mean the world to me, and I love you dearly.

I would like to thank my pastors, Kirbyjon and Suzette Caldwell, for their unyielding support. You both rallied the entire Windsor Village Church family behind my family and me and this case. Encouraging and inspiring to say the least, you have continued to exemplify exceptional leadership. I am proud and grateful to be under your tutelage.

It has always been kind of funny to me to think about how certain relationships have formed. If I hadn't been at this place, or answered this email, or stopped to say hello to this person, then this or that door would have never opened. Over the years, people who've paraded around as supporters and made empty promises to help have come and gone. But I've noticed that with the people who are really supposed to be in my life, there's always some crazy story about a perfect storm of events that brought us together; that's nothing but God all up and through there. It has been a long lonely lesson, but I have learned to trust and appreciate the process. Everything happened exactly the way it was supposed to and I am a gratitude machine to all of those who follow:

To my incredible agent Jan Miller, I thank God for you every day. As I was writing my thank yous, I had about twenty or thirty adjectives to describe your awesomeness, but I can't think of anything more perfect to call you than what you are: an angel. Thank you for being the dopest ever! I love you. Austin Miller, thank you so much for your help, guidance, and calming presence, and most of all your patience. I know at times I had to have bugged the hell out of you with questions, but you never made me feel that way and always encouraged me to reach out. Bless you, brother! Like it or not, you're stuck with a lifelong friend. Lacy (LL Cool) Lynch, thank you for all your help and support. When I was nervous as hell in those meetings in New York, you encouraged me and made me believe I belonged there. And thank you to the entire Dupree Miller family for your support and being so kind to me when I crashed the office.

Much love to Lawrence Ross for your hard work and commitment to this book. From the moment we met and sat down at the Starbucks in Corona, California, I knew this would be a great book. We sat for hours talking about the project, and life, and music; it was like talking to a friend. I'm inspired by your passion for the black voice and telling the world about the black experience. Thank you, my brother, for your wisdom, your patience, and your professionalism.

To Kate Hartson, Grace Johnson, and the whole team at Center Street and Hachette Book Group, thank you. Thank you for giving me an opportunity to tell my story to the world.

To Pastor Marvin Winans, I thank you for your spirit. When we met in Houston, you told my mom and me that you wouldn't forget about us and that you would not stop telling our story, and my goodness, you kept your word and told my story to THE Jan Miller, and here we are. Bless you, man of God!

To Martin Siegel, I cannot say enough good things about you. To work diligently for over a year on a case that was deemed a long shot, without a single dollar, speaks volumes about your character. I thank you. My family thanks you. And I'm sure all of the families that have used YOUR Supreme Court case, *Tolan v. Cotton*, thank you. To the dream team: Darryl Parks, Darryl Washington, Nick Pittman, Natalie Jackson, Matthew Pita,

Shaundala Brown, Jennifer Morgan, and, saving the best for last, Ben Crump. Thank you all for your time and dedication to this cause and to this case! Ben, thank you for being such a champion for civil rights and the conduit to the national spotlight for these families in turmoil. I'll never forget you sitting at the kitchen table at my parents' house and saying, "As a black attorney, civil rights is in your DNA." I greatly admire you, and I'm honored to have your support, your ear, and your friendship.

Thank you Bryant Gumbel, David Scott, and the whole HBO *Real Sports* crew. Thank you all for your kindness and your candidness in sharing my story with the world. I am forever grateful. To the Investigation Discovery family—Henry, Koz, Reenie, Jessica, and Asena—thank you all for being so kind to my family and me. From TCA to The Paley Center to the screening in Houston, each event was a blast. Thank you for keeping my story alive with your platform. You guys are awesome! Finally, to my man Keith Beauchamp, I thank you for your persistence, brother. Thank you for your passion for civil rights and social justice. We have to get back on tour soon, man! Thank you for your friendship.

My boys Eric, Jason, Chris, DJ, I love y'all to life. Oh, the stories we have, lol. Thank you all for your boundless support and always being a phone call away to lend an ear or a shoulder. Dmitri, playing for you was one of the most enjoyable times of my life. Thank you for being cool as fuck. Thank you, DY, for your compassion and for your friendship. In New York, I told my story to a friend, expecting nothing in return, but you gave me an escape and an opportunity to once again play the game I love. I love you for that, brother. To my teammates PJ, Juice, Des (and the Jones boys), KK, and Bobby Ray, you all are the shit. It was an absolute honor to grind beside you guys. Thank you to the Gwynn (and extended) family; rest well, Big T. This is hella nerve-racking; I hope I'm not leaving anyone out. Thank you Dennis Gilbert, Barry Larkin, Darnell Coles, and Tony Tarasco. Shout out to the Destin/Cooperstown/Turks and Caicos crew. Dequina, I'm still waiting to create some more magic with you. I know it's coming, but thank you for your endless support and always encouraging me to create and be great. Crichelle, Slat Daddy, Ahmed, Eb, Cory, Amir, Dre Evans, Steve, Dixon, Courtlove, Bacon, and Nick, Stacey, and Myia, thank you for being you and having my back. I am blessed beyond measure to have all of you in my corner. I pray that God continues to bless everything you touch.

To the Houston Astros Youth Academy crew, Darryl Wade and Duane Stelly, thank you for your patience and understanding. I appreciate you all for the opportunity. Darryl, I've been taking donations to buy you some longer shorts, and we're almost at our goal. Those shorts are coming soon, my man! To the Cruuuuuuuuuuuuuz Baseball family: Rocky and Enrique, thank you both so much for allowing me to join your organization as a coach. I heard the tales of the '99 State Championship team and came to Bellaire High School as a freshman admiring the hell out of you guys. Fast forward 10+ years later and coaching side by side with you all has been the coolest. So to Rodrigo, Enrique "Fowler," Cochise, Revo, JD, and our powerhouse softball team... Good Shales! Love you guys!

Lastly, I beg again for forgiveness from anyone who has supported me over the years whose name I have failed to mention. Please judge my mind and not my heart. Your presence and encouragement are, and always have been, remarkable and invaluable.

# INDEX

# ABOUT THE AUTHORS

**Robbie Tolan** is a prominent voice of the millennial generation, having been thrust into the national debate over police brutality after having been shot by a Bellaire, Texas (Houston suburb), police officer in 2008. Prior to this, Tolan followed in the baseball footsteps of his father, former Major League Baseball player Bobby Tolan, who played in the MLB for fourteen years and played in four World Series before moving his family to Houston, Texas. Robbie played in the minor leagues for the Washington Nationals before his career was cut short by the police shooting.

Tolan has appeared in numerous publications, including *The New York Times, Associated Press,* and *Essence Magazine.* He was also featured on *The Injustice Files* on Investigation Discovery, MSNBC with Melissa Harris-Perry, and HBO's *Real Sports with Bryant Gumbel,* where his story sparked international outrage. Since then, Robbie Tolan has spent the past decade fighting for the rights of black victims seeking justice when dealing with police officers and the judicial system. His law-making case, *Tolan v. Cotton*, has set the precedent in the way judges are allowed to grant police officers qualified immunity. Since its ruling in 2014,

01/2018